WITH DIVERSITY

A Portrait of the
Colne Group
of
Lowestoft

Compiled by
MALCOLM
WHITE

Proceeds from the sale of this book
will be donated to maritime charities

Front Cover Photograph - This impressive view of *LT62 St. Martin* undertaking sea trials off the Dutch coast was recorded in 1991. A unit of the present Lowestoft fleet, she was delivered to her home port on the 17th November 1991. In 1997 and 1998, under Skipper J. Jonas, she was the top trawler. Her hull was constructed in Poland, she has a German engine and the vessel was completed in Holland. Her sister ship, the *St. Matthew,* was also completed in 1991, but has a hull constructed in Yugoslavia.

Title Page Photograph - *LT122 Bermuda* was truly a special vessel. She was the first new build for any Colne company, and marked an important development stage for the Group. *Bermuda* was completed in 1955 by Cochrane and Sons Ltd. at Selby, and was powered by a 6cyl Ruston. In 1956, she was top trawler at Lowestoft under Skipper Newbury. In the later years of her life, she was used on offshore standby duties, and in June 1980 left Lowestoft for the last time, bound for a shipbreakers yard and cutting up. *Bermuda* is seen here leaving Lowestoft on a fishing trip in the early years of her life, with two members of the crew preparing to hoist the sail.

Back Cover Photograph (Left) - This 1948 colour photograph shows *PD388 Equity I* off Lowestoft undergoing trials. This drifter/trawler was built on "spec" by Brooke Marine Ltd., and launched as the *Madame Prunier.* She was completed for the Scottish Cooperative Society Ltd. as *Equity I.* Her frames, planking and beams were all made of English oak and the decking was of Oregon pine. She was powered by a 265hp Crossley diesel. A vessel that was in the Colne fleet for less than two years, she was very similar to the many former Admiralty Motor Fishing Vessels, which were in the fleet for many years. *Equity I* regained her original name whilst in the Colne fleet and was sold in 1953 as the *Madame Prunier.*

Back Cover Photograph (Right) - One of the impressive 300 Hospital Class standby vessels, the *St. Luke,* leaves Lowestoft on the 31st March 1979. Formerly the distant water trawler *LO65 Robert Hewett,* she was built in 1961 by Cook, Welton and Gemmell at Beverley. In common with other vessels of the standby fleet, she was later painted high visibility orange. *St. Luke* was in the Colne fleet from 1978 until 1992, when she was sold, and continued to be used as a standby vessel by her new owner.

Note

Every effort has been made to ensure the information in this book is accurate. For this reason, official documentation backed up by the author's own diaries and other local records have been consulted for factual support. However, when considering such a complex and variable subject with many thousands of intricate details, 100% accuracy cannot be guaranteed

Charities that will benefit from the sale of this book are as follows: -

Royal National Mission To Deep Sea Fishermen (RNMDSF)

The Lowestoft Fisherman's and Seafarers' Benevolent Society

Lowestoft & East Suffolk Maritime Heritage Museum

Published by	Malcolm R. White, 71 Beeching Drive, Denes Park, Lowestoft, Suffolk, NR32 4TB England, United Kingdom.
First Published	June 2000
Copyright	© Malcolm R. White 2000
ISBN	0 9532485 2 6

Printed by	Micropress Printers Ltd., 27 Norwich Road, Halesworth, Suffolk, IP19 8BX, England, United Kingdom.

CONTENTS

Page

ACKNOWLEDGEMENTS

The sources of information that have enabled this review and comprehensive fleet list to be prepared are many. The great majority of the information has come from various sources of official documentation and personal reports. A number of past and present Colne personnel, both sea going and shore staff have provided valuable contributions through recollections of events.

As with previous projects, the two principal societies dedicated to preserving and recording the fishing and general maritime heritage of Lowestoft and the surrounding area provided support and assistance. These societies are the Port of Lowestoft Research Society (PLRS), and its sister society, the Lowestoft & East Suffolk Maritime Society (LESMS).The LESMS is responsible for the provision and maintenance of the Lowestoft & East Suffolk Maritime Heritage Museum.

The following organisations, companies and representatives of companies have provided greatly appreciated assistance and co-operation. In some cases, I have been allowed to use material for which they own the copyright.

Waveney Advertiser	Associated British Ports	Robert Catchpole
Putford Enterprises	Hugh Sims	David White
Fishing News	Elizabeth White	Terry Reeve
Tim Oliver	George Prior Engineering	Tate and Lyle
Small & Co. (Engineering)	W. Stevenson & Sons	Flying Focus
British Trawler Federation	The Colne Shipping Co. Ltd.	

The Skipper and Crew of LT1005 St. Anthony: -

Skipper	Roly Reynolds
Mate	Gavin Athorn
Chief Engineer	Jimmy Tusting
Deckhand	John Cooke
Deckhand	Graham Crickmore
Deckhand	Clifford Warren

The work carried out by Sue Goodwin has been much valued. Sue sought and provided many valuable details of the Group and its vessels, previously known to very few people. My gratitude is extended to her for her endeavours.

I am grateful to John Wells and his staff for help and assistance with archive material used in this publication. Access to the extensive John Wells Heritage Collection has enabled many superb period photographs to be included in the photographic review. Many classic images captured by John over several years are to be found throughout the book.

The assistance and support of Neil Watson has enabled many varied aspects of Colne Shipping to be featured. Neil recorded the scenes through the lens of his camera over a period of several years, and these provide an impressive portrait of the company and many aspects of the Lowestoft fishing industry. In addition to the special feature highlighting Neil's work, his photographs can also be found on pages three and eight. My thanks to Neil for supplying all the photographs, and taking so much time and trouble in recording and providing these views.

Much appreciated has been the interest in the project from Eric and Jean Baker, Hans Boje, Stanley Earl, Peter Hansford, Frank and Ena Howes, Thelma Jones, Ken Kent, LESMS Chairman Peter Parker, and my fellow officers of the PLRS.

Valuable input via the PLRS Newsletters has been provided by Alan Page. For editorial support, I am very much indebted to Stuart Jones BA., formerly of CEFAS Laboratory, Lowestoft.

PHOTOGRAPHIC OWNERSHIP AND COPYRIGHT

The vast number of photographs used in this publication come from many sources, the author took many and some are from his collection. In addition to those mentioned in the previous column, with their kind permission, the following hold copyright for photographs that are included in this book: -

Scottish Fisheries Museum, Lowestoft & East Suffolk Maritime Society, Port of Lowestoft Research Society, Gordon Birney, Peter Calvert, Ken Carsey, Stanley Earl, Pamela Graystone, Peter Hansford, Ernest Harvey, Ken Kent and Peter Killby.

Other books in the Coastal and Maritime Series by Malcolm White . . . . .

DOWN THE HARBOUR 1955-1995
40 years of fishing vessels, owners, the harbour and shipyards at Lowestoft
ISBN 09532485 0 X

A CENTURY OF FISHING
Fishing from Gt.Yarmouth and Lowestoft
ISBN 09532485 1 8

Web Site: www.MaritimeLowestoft.co.uk
E-mail: Books@MaritimeLowestoft.co.uk

LT333 Fertile

Many people do not associate steam-powered vessels with Colne and Mr. G. Claridge. The *Fertile*, a steam drifter purchased by Mr. G. Claridge in 1946, is seen here leaving Lowestoft complete with the well known houseflag on her funnel. This 1907 built vessel was one of several steam drifters owned by the Colne group of companies. These played a vital part in the development and later modernisation of the fleet; the great majority of the steam-powered vessels that were owned by the Group are featured in this book. *Fertile* is passing the well-known Lowestoft dredgers *Pioneer* and *Progress;* both built in the 1880s by Pearce at Stockton on Tees.

Mr. Gordon Claridge

The Colne Group's founder, Mr. Gordon Claridge, at just two of the great many presentations that he attended.
(Above) On the occasion of General Manager Aubrey Moore's retirement in 1981.
Left Photograph
(Left to Right) Gordon Claridge, Aubrey Moore, John Leggett, Evelyn Moore, Mrs Weekes, Margaret Leggett, John Balls, Harold Weekes, John Balls, Frank E. Howes.
Right Photograph
(Left to Right) John Leggett, Thelma Jones, Skipper Ernie Peek, Ships Husband Charlie Page, Gordon Claridge, Skipper John Peek, Aubrey Moore, Mrs Weekes, Harold Weekes
(Bottom Left) On the occasion of Diesel Fitter Frank Howes retirement in August 1979.
(Left to Right) George Cooper, Margaret Leggett, Gordon Claridge, Frank Howes, Ena Howes, Bob Hovells, John Balls

INTRODUCTION

To the British fishing industry, the latter half of the 20th century brought about many changes. The disappearance of long established fisheries, the loss of traditional fishing grounds, and the introduction of seemingly endless rules and regulations saw major restructuring taking place. During this period, many well known fishing companies operating from various fishing ports around the country withdrew from the industry completely, or ceased trading due to financial reasons. Substantial numbers of fishing vessels were disposed of, reducing the British fishing fleet to a shadow of its former self.

One of the major operators of fishing vessels to survive this turbulent period has been **The Colne Shipping Co. Ltd**., set up in the early 1980s. The origins of this company and it's predecessors date back to the mid 1940s, when Mr. Gordon Claridge commenced operations at Lowestoft. Once established, the group of companies operating under the Colne umbrella grew to become the largest privately owned concern of its type in the United Kingdom. Later, in the 1970s and 1980s, the group had a very large number of vessels engaged in supporting the offshore oil and gas industry.

At the start of the 21st century, Colne Shipping remains one of the major owners of fishing vessels in this country, operating a fleet of modern large beam trawlers out of Lowestoft. The company is a much-respected driving force within the industry. Survival of this diverse company is largely due to good tactical planning, flexibility and perseverance by its directors and managers supported by a dedicated workforce at sea and on shore.

The presence of the Colne group of companies in Lowestoft has provided substantial economic benefit to the town and port for many years, and is today, largely responsible for maintaining Lowestoft as a modern major British fishing port. This book considers those companies, vessels and interests of the Colne group that have been involved in fishing, offshore work and other maritime related industries.

Regretfully, a great many people even in Lowestoft are totally unaware of the modern fishing industry, the vessels, and the way of life on board them. Some prefer to visualise the fishing industry as Scottish fisher girls working at the farlins, during the home fishing in days gone by. Others have images from the past of the harbour full of fishing vessels, grossly inefficient by present day economic standards. This is no longer relevant, and is more suited to preservation in the maritime museum.

This book is intended as a specialised fishing and maritime heritage publication, and it is assumed that the reader has an appreciation of the British fishing industry. Imperial measures have been used throughout.

Additional information and further photographs of vessels belonging to the Colne group of companies are to be found in the two previous books in this maritime heritage series.

Malcolm White
Lowestoft
June 2000

Colne Shipping
1999

The management team of Colne Shipping in 1999
(Left to Right) Company Secretary Hugh Sims, Operations Manager Andy Bagshaw,
Engineering Manager Keith Holland, Safety Officer Ian Colby
Seated-General Manager Courtney Clark, Managing Director Robin Claridge

The Colne organisation in Lowestoft can trace its origins back to 1945, when Mr. Gordon David Claridge commenced operations as a trawler owner in the town. Initially operating just two fishing vessels, the steam drifter/trawler *Lass O' Doune* and the small diesel trawler *Ala*, Mr. Claridge soon set about expanding his fleet. Two more vessels were purchased in the following year, these being the *Guava,* and the *Gula,* a sister ship of the *Ala*. A further five vessels were added to the fleet in 1947, and each of the years from 1948 until 1961 saw additions being made to the fleet.

During the early 1950s, a number of the vessels in the Colne fleet were former Admiralty 90 foot MFVs known locally as "Wooden Wonders", or "Wooden Clumpers". Vessels such as *Snapper, Albacore, Aylesby, Enderby, Grasby* and *Eta* were all of this standard wartime design. These vessels were wonderful sea boats, but it was generally accepted that their engines made them rather under powered for trawling. However, they helped consolidate the Group before the start of the new building programme, which commenced in 1954 with the *Bermuda*.

For the first four years, Mr. Claridge personally owned all the vessels; however in 1949 two companies were formed. These companies were the Colne Fishing Co. Ltd., the parent Company of the Group, and Claridge Trawlers Ltd. Many of the vessels owned by Mr. Claridge were transferred to these companies shortly after their formation. Three Grimsby fishing companies were taken over and added to the Group during the following years, namely Huxley Fishing Co. Ltd. in 1951, Clan Steam Fishing Co. (Grimsby) Ltd. in 1952 and the Dagon Fishing Co. Ltd. in 1955. A further acquisition was the Milford Haven firm of Drifter Trawlers Ltd. in 1957. By 1961, the fleet was run and arranged on a company basis and had grown into one of the largest, if not the largest, privately owned trawler fleet in the United Kingdom. The number of vessels in the Colne fleet continued to grow for many years, initially all being employed on fishing. Until 1975, the two principal methods of fishing by vessels owned by the Group had been drift net fishing by the drifters in the fleet and trawling by side-fishing trawlers. During 1975 however, two new stern trawlers were delivered, the first and last of this type of vessel to be owned by the Group.

By the middle of the 1980s, a policy decision had been taken to invest in beam trawling and a number of beam trawlers were acquired, mainly from Dutch owners. This decision brought about the rapid demise of the side and stern trawlers in the fleet, and some of these vessels were disposed of. The majority however, ceased fishing and transferred to work associated with the offshore oil and gas industry. Since the 1960s, the Colne Group had become increasingly involved in the search for oil and gas in the North Sea. This involvement led to a demand for many vessels, and by 1981, the combined fishing and offshore support fleet exceeded 100. All of these were either owned or operated by the Group, the parent company of which became The Colne Shipping Co. Ltd., the following year.

In the late 1980s, and during the 1990s, orders were placed with continental shipyards for a number of new beam trawlers, and these remain in service today. It has become normal practice for major sections of these vessels to be constructed in various eastern European countries. These sections are then taken to Holland, and final assembly of the vessel is carried out there. The most recent of these large beam trawlers is the *St. Anthony*, delivered in March 1999. A typical fishing trip for these vessels lasts twelve days. With a far greater catching capacity and a substantial reduction in the manpower requirement, these vessels are significantly more cost effective than their predecessors were. This fact is often overlooked when comparisons are made between the fishing fleets of today, and those of bygone days.

The vast majority of the vessels owned by the Colne Group have been diesel powered. The impression held in some quarters is that Mr. Claridge and the Colne group of companies owned few steam powered vessels. In fact between 1945 and 1957, the various operating companies within the Group owned a total of nine steam drifter/ trawlers. In a few cases, the steam vessels were acquired when the owning Company was taken over and thus became part of the Colne Group. Many of these vessels were retained for only a few years before being sold for scrapping, some under the Government "Scrap and Build" scheme for building new vessels. However, some were units of the Colne fleet for many years, such as the former Peterhead steam drifter *Fertile*, a member of the fleet from late 1946 until 1954.

VESSEL MANAGEMENT

The management of the Group's vessels was undertaken in the earliest days by two existing Lowestoft fishing vessel managers, East Coast Fish Sales Ltd. and Boston Deep Sea Fishing & Ice Co. Ltd. During the mid 1950's however, the Colne Group took over East Coast Fish Sales Ltd., and the management of all the vessels in the Group was transferred to that Company. When they were first acting as managers of some of Mr. Claridge's fleet, East Coast Fish Sales Co. Ltd. were also managers of vessels for other owners. This included some owners new to the port, and others formed to buy old vessels and get them fishing again. These included the Raw Material Supply Corporation Ltd., R. G. Parsley,

Cranbrook Shipping Co. Ltd., Cranley Shipping Co. Ltd., Resondo Trawlers Ltd. and the Jubilee Fishing Co. Ltd. The vessels included *Caspian, Grosbeak, Dereske, Warren, Vera Creina, Leonard, Ipswich, Landbreeze, Capetown* and *Saxmundham*. These, and a great many like them, have been broken up long ago but they certainly played their part in the re-building of the trawl fishing industry at Lowestoft in the immediate post war period.

For a number of years East Coast Fish Sales had an office at Fleetwood and managed those Colne vessels that operated from there. By December 1967, the office had closed, and Dalby Steam Fishing Co. Ltd. then undertook the management of any Colne vessel working from the Lancashire port. One of the last Colne vessels to operate from Fleetwood when the Company had their own office there, was *LT326 Yellowtail*. However, many years have passed since a Colne fishing vessel worked out of Fleetwood. In addition to Lowestoft and Fleetwood, vessels of the Colne Group have made landings at other ports such as Milford Haven and Grimsby. Their vessels have also landed in Holland. Management of the present fleet is carried out under the umbrella of Colne Shipping.

OFFSHORE SUPPORT

Following the discovery of gas and oil in the North Sea by the mid 1960s, and later in other areas, a safety and standby requirement existed in the offshore industry. Vessels were to be stationed at all times in the vicinity of all manned rigs and platforms, to be able to provide rapid response in any emergency situation on or near the structures.

By the late 1960s, the Group had diversified and had become involved in this work, initially utilising some of the older vessels in their fleet. Trawlers and drifter/trawlers were thought suitable for this new role and initially little work was carried out on these vessels before they commenced offshore work. For a few years before they were sold for scrapping in 1968, *British Guiana* and *British Honduras* became two of the first Colne vessels to be used on this work. Later, new standards were introduced and major conversion work was carried out on any vessel which was to be used for this work. Such was the demand, that within a few years it became necessary for the Group to buy and convert a large number of trawlers from other ports. Many trawlers previously never seen at Lowestoft started working from the port as offshore standby vessels.

During 1977, Lloyds List carried an interesting article on offshore safety and standby vessels. In the article it was stated that: "Colne Fishing Co. Ltd. has rapidly acquired by far the largest share of the North Sea standby market in the six years since the Company first diversified into this part of the offshore business". At that time, 58 Colne vessels were employed on this work operating out of Fleetwood, Aberdeen and Lowestoft for Amoco, BP, British Gas, Conoco, Placid, Saga, Shell UK, SunOil and Texaco. The 37 contracts held included the U.K., Norwegian and Dutch sectors of the North Sea and offshore Ireland. During this period, Colne Fishing was at the forefront of providing spraying equipment on their vessels to deal with oil spills at sea. Some of the first vessels with this equipment included the five on charter to J. Marr & Sons, and three of the fleet operating out of Lowestoft. A programme existed to rapidly upgrade the remainder of the fleet.

Classification of the standby vessels depended upon their size, and the resources and accommodation that they could provide in case of an emergency. Colne vessels were grouped into a number of classes the principal ones being the 100, 150, 250, and the 300 Class vessels. Examples of these classes of vessels were: -

100 Class - *Sawfish*	150 Class - *Pagona,*
250 Class - *SSAFA*	300 Class - *St. Louis*

The 250 Class vessels were referred to as the 250 North Atlantic Survivor Class standby vessels, and the 300 Class vessels as the 300 Hospital Class standby vessels. During the early 1980s, vessels of the 250 Class could be found at work out in the Atlantic and in the South Western Approaches supporting companies such as Chevron and working with the semi-submersible rig, *Benvrackie*. Vessels of the 300 Class were equipped with hospital treatment facilities. The first of the 300 Class vessels, the *St. Davids*, cost over £750,000 in 1981- 82 to conceive, design, convert and equip. Within days of her entering service in June 1982, she rescued a man who had been thrown into the sea from a workboat near the *Thistle A* Platform, using one of her two Arctic 22 rescue boats.

The range of activities and the area for which Colne were responsible became extensive, extending from the Hewett and Leman Bank Gas fields, to the most northerly operations above the Shetlands. An associated Company, Irish Standby Boats Ltd., covered the operations from Ireland. Vessels operating through that Company included many of the 250 class. These supported operations by Phillips Petroleum and Esso Exploration, west of Ireland in the Atlantic.

By 1982, the offshore standby fleet included several large former distant water trawlers previously fishing from Hull, Grimsby and Fleetwood. Many famous vessels such as the *Arctic Rebel, Arctic Vandal, Lord Jellicoe, Lord St. Vincent, Northern Reward, Northern Gift, Ella Hewett* and *Robert Hewett* joined the Lowestoft fleet. Some of these impressive vessels were well known from their encounters with Icelandic gunboats during the Cod Wars. The gunboats were attempting to stop trawlers fishing by ramming and wire cutting. After conversion these vessels formed the 300 Class fleet.

The British National Oil Corporation working the Thistle field, had been a customer of Colne since 1978. The contract was renewed in the mid 1980s with the work being entrusted to the 300 Class vessels. In addition, during this period the Company added Chevron Petroleum UK to the impressive list of offshore companies, for which it was supplying safety and standby services. The contract awarded by Chevron was to supply standby vessels to cover their northern, southern and central Ninian fields. This work required the use of a further three vessels, two of the 250 survivor class and one of the 300 class. Meanwhile, 300 miles out in the Atlantic in very hostile conditions, Colne vessels such as the *St. Mark*, were providing standby services to the drilling ship *Discoverer Seven Seas*. This drilling ship was on charter to the British National Oil Corporation, and was involved in the deepest ever drilling programme.

The offshore standby work developed into a major undertaking for the group and at one time over 70 Company vessels were assigned to it. For many years, substantial contracts continued to be awarded to the Company, together with the renewal of others. In some cases, the work was sub-contracted to companies such as British United Trawlers (BUT), and J. Marr & Son. This involved vessels such as *Benella, Edwina*, and *Ross Khartoum*. The standby vessels of the Colne Group of companies could be found almost anywhere around the British Isles where the various oil and gas companies were operating. This necessitated the setting up of a major supply and support organisation by the Company. In 1982, to transport crews and other personnel around the various ports, Colne Shipping bought a 14 seater Mercedes 508D coach. Soon it had proved its worth and was travelling over 7000 miles each month.

Two new operational bases were opened in 1982, one at Fleetwood and the other at Plymouth. These provided base port facilities to standby vessels working in near waters. In Fleetwood, the operational base was established in conjunction with John Ward & Sons to support such vessels as *Exuma, Anegada* and *Bermuda* at that time servicing two jack-up rigs, *Apollo II* and *Arch Rowan*. In Plymouth, the base was set up in association with W. Tamlyn & Son. This base supported the 250 Class vessels working in the South Western Approaches and the Irish sector.

New minimum standards for offshore and safety standby vessels were set out in a Department of Energy report in 1981, superseding those issued in 1975/6. The *Piper Alpha* disaster and the following investigation of the incident by Lord Cullen saw new regulations being introduced, and existing standards upgraded. The health and safety issue was paramount and included in the new regulations were amended requirements for vessels involved in standby work. These called for vessels to be of a higher calibre and capability, and set a time scale for the implementation of the new standards. By the early 1990s, the smaller standby vessels had been withdrawn and most sold for scrapping. A few however, were sold for further use and one the *Togo,* has visited her former home port in recent years in her new role as a charter vessel.

The large former distant water trawlers in the fleet by now fitted with bow thrusters continued in use, together with the two former stern trawlers built for the Company in 1975. In later years, these were sold to a separate Company, Colne Standby Ltd. This Company was set up by Bruce Claridge and had no connection with Colne Shipping except for buying the remaining large standby vessels from them.

Vessels of the Colne Fishing standby fleet were involved in many rescues. For example in the spring of 1981, there were four; the *SSAFA* working well out in the Atlantic rescued 14 members of the crew of a sinking Spanish trawler. The *Trinidad* working off the Shetlands picked up a man, who had fallen off a platform, the rescue was completed in 4 minutes. Another similar rescue in the Brent field, well beyond the Shetlands, involved the *Antigua* and occurred in 45-knot winds and waves of 16 feet. Also during that spring, the *Exuma,* picked up the crew of a sinking Danish cargo ship a few miles from the West Sole gas field. The coaster passed close to Platform *48-6-A*, which had to be shutdown and evacuated, and eventually sank 25 miles east of Spurn Head. These are just a few examples of the excellent work carried out by Colne vessels and their crews. Often oil companies made presentations to the crews of the vessels involved in the rescues, as in the case of the rescues by the *Antigua* and *Trinidad*.

Many people underestimate the major contribution that the Colne group of companies made to the exploration of the North Sea and other waters from the late 1960s into the 1990s. Today the Colne Shipping Group is no longer involved in this work.

OTHER COMPANY VESSELS

Over the years, Colne Shipping and the preceding companies have owned a succession of tugs. These have been the *Mardyke, Ala,* and two named *Eta*. In the past, the main use of these tugs has been to move fishing vessels around the port. The present tug is the second to be named *Eta*. This well kept useful vessel undertakes general towage work around the port, in addition to supporting the beam trawlers of the fleet. On numerous occasions she has visited Great Yarmouth to work, usually to assist the port tug *Hector Read* with difficult operations. During August 1999, *Eta* appeared before an estimated crowd of 90,000 people when she had a starring role off the South Beach at Lowestoft, during the second day of the annual Air Show. Never have so many people watched a vessel of the Colne fleet in action.

VESSEL LOSSES

The Colne Group has been in existence for over 50 years, and during that time, has owned over 150 vessels. It is a tribute to the calibre of the officers and crews employed by the companies within the Group, that relatively few vessels have been lost at sea. More importantly, the loss of life and serious injury sustained on Colne vessels since 1945, has been low considering the hostile and appalling conditions that the vessels have worked in.

The first vessel lost was the *Lass O' Doune* in 1947, whilst on passage from the West Coast to Lowestoft. She sank off the Sussex coast. The next vessel lost was the *Aylesby*; she caught fire and sank in the North Sea during 1951. On the 31st January 1953, the *Guava* went missing in severe weather with 11 men aboard. She had left Lowestoft the previous day to trawl for herring on the Sandette grounds. The findings of the Court of Inquiry, set up to investigate her loss were that: "she had been suddenly overwhelmed by the force of the wind, and the high confused state of the sea". No trace of the vessel, a former minesweeper, was found.

In 1957, the trawler *British Columbia* sank in the North Sea after a collision with an American destroyer. A number of years were to pass before the next vessel would be lost. This was the tug *Mardyke*, which ran aground in December 1973, whilst attempting to tow the standby vessel *Grenada* off the Corton Sands. During 1974, the standby vessel *Grayfish* became a total loss after running ashore on the Shetlands, later she broke in two. During May 1978, the *St.Luke* sank following an explosion. The *Cuttlefish* was lost after grounding off north Norfolk in November 1981. *Spearfish*, a vessel similar to the *Grayfish* and the *Cuttlefish*, became a navigational hazard after a collision during 1983. The Royal Navy sank her with gunfire. The next loss occurred during January 1986, when the tug *Ala* capsized and sank off Lowestoft.

During the last ten years, only two vessels have been lost. These were both involved in offshore standby work, the *St. Mark* sank after a collision off the north Norfolk coast in 1990, and the *St. Martin* sank off the Lincolnshire coast in 1991.

ORGANISATION, SUBSIDIARIES AND DIVERSITY

The long-standing head office of the Group is located at Waveney Road in Lowestoft, from where it overlooks the Trawl Dock. In addition to the fishing vessel managing company, and the various fishing vessel owning companies already mentioned, the Group has a number of subsidiary companies involved in maritime related activities at Lowestoft. These all serve other industries and trades in addition to the fishing industry. LBS Engineering, Lowestoft Ice Co. and East Coast Oil Wharves are three of these companies. The wide range of facilities, services and expertise existing within the Group, means that it has been virtually self-sufficient for many years. It is able to provide in house, almost all the required services and maintenance requirements that it needs. On the 1st April 1982, in order to reflect more accurately the diverse nature of the Group, the parent Company became The Colne Shipping Co. Ltd. At that time, in addition to fishing, a major commitment of the Group was providing safety and standby services to offshore oil and gas companies. This involvement in offshore support lasted until the early 1990s. Since then the core business of the Group is again fishing. Today, Colne can boast one of the largest privately owned and most modern fleets in the UK fishing industry, supported by subsidiary companies working in the associated fields.

LBS Engineering Co. Ltd. is a well-known local firm of engineers and ship repairers, acquired by the Colne Group in 1962. Founded at their Hamilton Road premises in 1930, they carried out the first steam to diesel conversion for the Lowestoft fishing fleet in 1935. This vessel was the former Yarmouth drifter/trawler *Togo*, which at that time had been purchased by Lowestoft owners. Later in life, she would become a unit of the Colne fleet. During the 1950s and early 1960s, this Company carried out many steam to diesel conversions. LBS Engineering has a large well-equipped machine shop, and can undertake most types of fabrication and heavy engineering. During April 1998, LBS Engineering vacated their prominent Hamilton Road premises and moved to the Colne Shipping base at Riverside Road in Lowestoft. This base was initially set up at the end of 1984, in what had been until 1962, part of the East Anglian Ice and Cold Storage Co. premises. Before moving to Riverside, the repair and refitting yard of the Colne Group had been at the western end of North Quay.

LBS undertake maintenance work at Riverside on Colne vessels, and contract work for fishing vessel owners and other customers.

East Coast Oil Wharves have their operating base at Hamilton Road in Lowestoft. From there, they carry out fuel distribution for many customers, in addition to supplying the Group requirements. Their roadtankers are frequently seen around the harbour area and further afield, satisfying customer's requirements. Vessels serviced include ocean going salvage tugs, survey vessels, safety supply and safety standby vessels, visiting fishing vessels, other port users and shipping visiting the port. Quayside bunkering facilities are also available. The fuel deliveries to Lowestoft come by sea, the coastal tankers discharging into the storage tanks in Hamilton Road via an underground transfer pipeline, from the tanker berth in the Outer Harbour.

The Lowestoft Ice Co. Ltd. was purchased from the Lowestoft Fishing Vessel Owners Association, during the autumn of 1984. At that time, the Ice Co. was producing about twenty five thousand tons of ice per year. Lowestoft Ice Co. Ltd.

can trace its origins back to the East Anglian Ice and Cold Storage Co. Ltd. whose works stood on the south bank of Lake Lothing. Head of that Company for many years was Mr. W. F. Cockrell who pioneered the development of the diesel-powered trawler in the 1930s. Mr. Cockrell is considered by many, as the person responsible for revolutionising the British fishing industry with this means of propulsion. Later, he became Chairman of the well-known Lowestoft shipbuilders Richards Ironworks Ltd. Built in 1962; the existing premises of the Lowestoft Ice Co. Ltd. are adjacent to the Waveney Dock. The Company manufactures and supplies ice not only for the fishing industry, but also food companies and for special events. On occasions, it has been known to supply ice to the building and construction industry. The Company also offers a number of specialised services and facilities.

GROUP COLOURS, MARKINGS AND LIVERY

Over the years, the colours and livery of the vessels owned by the Group have seen a number of changes. All the trawlers in the present fleet have their hulls painted dark blue, with red boot topping. Earlier colour schemes for trawlers have seen the hulls painted black with a white line; this was later phased out and replaced by grey, but retaining the white line. With this grey colour scheme, the fishing registration on the vessels had a black background. The steam and diesel powered drifters, and drifter/trawlers all had a black hull. Initially, the large number of vessels used as offshore standby vessels continued to carry the basic colours of fishing vessels. In later years, partly due to the increased safety awareness within the offshore industry, the topsides of these vessels were painted high visibility orange.

Tugs owned by Colne, including the present *Eta,* have all had a black hull and red boot topping.

The markings and colours used on the funnels and exhaust uptakes of the vessels owned by Mr. Gordon Claridge and the many subsidiary companies have changed over the years. An early colour scheme for the fishing vessels included a very large white "C" on a blue funnel with a black top. Another had three wide coloured bands on the funnel, the top band black, the middle band white and the bottom band blue. The white band included a very large black "C".

For a great many years however, the funnel or engine exhaust uptake of all vessels including the tugs and offshore safety and standby vessels, has been blue with a black top. Where space permitted the Company houseflag was displayed on the funnel or uptake. If space was limited, the houseflag was usually located on the outside of the skipper's cabin aft of the wheelhouse, and immediately below the funnel. The houseflag generally used was white with a blue "C" in the centre. In recent years, a number of the beam trawlers have had the houseflag displayed on the side of the wheelhouse or casing with the colours reversed, resulting in a blue flag with a white "C" in the centre. After completion in 1975, and for several years after that, the two stern trawlers carried unique Company markings. On these vessels, the usual houseflag was replaced by a large blue "C" with rippled blue lines above and below. This was displayed on the each side of the wheelhouse under the middle window. After conversion for offshore standby work in the late 1980s, these non-standard markings were replaced by the usual houseflag mounted on the exhaust uptakes.

Road vehicles belonging to companies within the Group generally have a livery consisting of various shades of blue. Two deviations are the tractor units of the road tankers, which are bright yellow, a small pickup that is red and a white van. The majority of these vehicles carry the white Company houseflag with a blue "C" in the centre. Buildings and property owned by the Colne group of companies have traditionally been decorated in various shades of blue.

PRESS RELEASES, THE MEDIA AND PUBLICITY

The Colne group of companies has traditionally caught the attention of the media. Perhaps the most sustained media attention was in 1953 when the trawler *Guava* was lost. An ex-Naval wooden minesweeper, she had a crew of 11, nine from Lowestoft and one each from Yarmouth and Gorleston. Her skipper was 41 year old George Fisher of 12a Tennyson Road, Lowestoft. The most devastating headline for many at that time was "Hope Abandoned for Guava", which appeared on the 20th February 1953. Not only did the loss make the headlines, but also the three-day inquiry held at the Royal Hotel during November 1953, resulted in extensive coverage.

In the 1960s and 1970s, the subject of attention was usually the seemingly continuous flow of newly built trawlers joining the Company fleet. Another regular topic for many years was the Company vessels landing record catches. A typical example of this was in November 1975, when the local newspaper headline was: "Trawler Has A Record First Trip". The trawler was *St.Patrick*; she had landed 598 kits that sold for £15,091.

On the 22nd December 1973, the subject of the news was somewhat different. The headline was: " Five Saved Off Stranded Tug". The *Grenada* heading out for another spell of standby work had run aground on Corton Sands. The tug sent to free her, the *Mardyke*, also ran aground and became a total loss.

People have always been rated very highly by the Company and on many occasions reports of retirements, presentations and personnel moves have appeared in the press. In 1981, it was reported that Mr. Aubrey Moore was retiring as General Manager of the Colne Fishing Co. and East Coast Fish Sales. He intended to remain as President of the LFVOA and a director of the British Fishing Federation. In March of that year, the headline was "Colne Men Move up". This report drew attention to the fact that Mr. John Leggett had been appointed the new General Manager of the Company, and Mr. John Balls the deputy General Manager.

The headlines continued to highlight the Company, its people and activities, events and achievements and kept it in the public eye. In recent years, with Colne being the only major fishing company at Lowestoft, it has taken an even higher profile and become very much the centre of attention in the town and the fishing industry generally. This attention no doubt reflects the importance to the town of the fishing industry in general, and Colne Shipping in particular.

In April 1992, the European Union (EU) announced that a quota scheme would be introduced on the amount of North Sea plaice that could be caught. This was the first time that this had happened, and directly affected the Company. The press reports focused on the economics of the Company acquiring new trawlers just before the EU announcement was made.

During November 1994, the Company made the headlines and was featured on TV, after announcing that many of their trawlers would be withdrawn from service and decommissioned. This was in accordance with the British Government scheme for reducing the size of the country's fishing fleet. The result of this, according to the press, was that initially 18 jobs would be lost at Lowestoft, with a great many more to follow in the service and associated industries, as further vessels were taken out of service. The top trawler at the port in 1987 and 1988, the *St. Christopher*, was one of those decommissioned and quickly broken up.

On several occasions, the media attention has returned to the important issue of changes in the amount of fish to be caught by trawlers of the Colne fleet, under the EU quota scheme. An example of this was in December 1998, when it was announced that the UK's 1999 quota for North Sea plaice would be increased to 102,000 tonnes, up 15% on the 1998 figure. On other occasions, the reverse has happened and a decrease in the quota has been declared.

The death was announced in January 1996 of Mr. Gordon Claridge at the age of 84 years. From the small beginnings in 1945, Mr. Claridge rose to become a major figure in the post war fishing industry not only at Lowestoft but also throughout the country. He became known for his tenacity and championship of the fishing industry's cause. Without his foresight and careful economic planning, there is little doubt that the fishing industry, the port and town of Lowestoft, would be very much the poorer today. As a mark of respect for Mr. Claridge, a one-minute silence was observed on the Fish Market at Lowestoft on Friday 12 January 1996, the day following his death. In memory of Mr. Claridge, a Colne Shipping trawler, the *Hannah Christine*, was renamed *Gordon David* in early April 1996.

In recent years, a number of well-known figures within the Company have retired and received the attention of the press. Amongst these have been Mr. Bob Hovells, Mr. Harry Moore, Mr. Richard Fiske and Mr. John Nightingale Mr. Hovells was formerly General Manager of The Colne Shipping Co. Ltd. "Harry's Lifelong Link At An End", was the headline marking the retirement as Engineering Manager of Mr. Moore. He retired after spending 38 years with the Company. Mr. Fiske was for many years one of the ports most respected trawler skippers. His achievements in fishing were reflected in the headline "Trawler Skipper's Champion Record" which was accompanied with a large colour photograph of Richard on the tug *Eta*. He spent much of his career with Small & Co. (Lowestoft) Ltd., where he skippered such vessels as *Suffolk Punch* and *Suffolk Chieftain.* After joining Colne in 1981, he skippered the stern trawlers *St.Phillp* and *St.Patrick.* With the *St. Patrick* in 1983, he smashed the trawler landing record at the port with a catch that sold for £34,405. Before officially retiring, Richard was skipper of the tug *Eta* aboard which he may still occasionally be seen. Mr. John Nightingale was foreman fitter; he started working for Colne in 1957 and retired in 1998.

During the spring of 1999, Colne Shipping received widespread publicity on television, radio and the newspapers when their new trawler *St.Anthony* arrived at her home port. The headlines of the local paper proclaimed: "£3m Hi-Tech Trawler Propels Fleet Into The New Millennium", and stated that the arrival of the vessel heralded a new era within the fishing industry. The Fisheries Minister Mr. Elliot Morley and the local MP Mr. Bob Blizzard visited the vessel, and were shown around by Mr. Robin Claridge and Mr. Hugh Sims. The trade magazines and newspapers gave the event worldwide attention and covered the delivery of the vessel in detail with full reviews, accompanied by technical reports and many photographs.

Following the widespread publicity concerning the *St. Anthony*, an interesting feature appeared in the local weekly newspaper when their reporter spent some time aboard her with the mate of the vessel, Mr. Gavin Athorn. This feature was an in-depth report of life on board a modern trawler, and the way members of the crew spend their time. It highlighted the technical expertise required by the present day crew member and the qualifications that are necessary for them to carry out their duties. An important point made during the interview with Gavin was that drastic changes have taken place in the industry, and there was a need to project the modern industry. The report indicated that the future was dependent upon cost-effective highly automated vessels with advanced digital technology, satellite navigation and communications, quality living conditions and a galley full of the latest food storage and cooking equipment. With increasing safety awareness within the fishing industry, the latest trawlers have closed circuit television cameras installed, with monitors at a number of locations. The report projected Colne Shipping as a dynamic organisation with a flexible outlook, able to adjust to market forces. It also reflected well on the modern Lowestoft fishing industry and the people who are involved in it.

The prospect of further regulation within the industry is unfortunately ever present. One rule in particular, the " Days At Sea Scheme", is a topic that the Company is violently opposed to.

Imposition of endless rules and regulations on a hard pressed fishing industry by Europe and the Common Fisheries Policy, made the headlines in January 1999. The report highlighted a speech made by Mr. Robin Claridge at the Colne annual dinner for skippers and management at the end of 1998. In addition to the universally disliked Days at Sea scheme, other issues such as satellite monitoring, the working time directive, the testing for power rating of engines and the increasing number of inspections were also mentioned by Mr. Claridge. The point was emphasised that whereas some governments in the European Union supported their fishing industry, little support seems to be forthcoming from the British Government.

Mr. Claridge's views are not just held locally, but shared by a great many people throughout the British fishing industry.

In the closing months of the Twentieth Century, local press and television gave considerable coverage to two events affecting the Company, one indirectly and the other directly. The first concerned a new type of electronic fish auction to be set up at Lowestoft by a Belgian company. The impression gained from these reports was that the traditional "shout" auctions would disappear. This was not the case, as Colne Shipping, by far the major supplier, continued to hold these for their landings, using their own auctioneer.

The second announcement in the last few days of December 1999 was by far the more important. It concerned the ongoing saga of changes to the EU fish quotas. Fortunately on this occasion, although witnessing a slight reduction, the changes did not make major inroads into the amount of plaice that could be caught by the Company's nine trawlers. On television and in the press, Company Secretary Mr. Hugh Sims, said that the company was relieved after hearing the news that the catching of plaice has not been drastically cut.

MANAGEMENT

The management team of Colne Shipping at the beginning of the 21st Century was as follows: -

Managing Director	Mr. Robin Claridge
General Manager	Mr. Courtney Clarke
Company Secretary	Mr. Hugh Sims
Engineering Manager	Mr. Keith Holland
Operations Manager	Mr. Andy Bagshaw
Safety Officer	Mr. Ian Colby

Although the total number of fishing vessels operated by Colne Shipping now comprises of only nine beam trawlers, it remains one of the largest British owned trawler fleets. The Group presently employs around 120 people. However, a great many more are reliant on Colne Shipping either directly or indirectly for their livelihood.

The Company seeks to ensure the continuity of supply of fish to the Lowestoft Fish Market, and to ensure continuation of the Lowestoft fishing industry and Colne Shipping.

Companies that have been or are part of the Colne Group, and are considered in this book

Clan Steam Fishing Co. (Grimsby) Ltd.	Vessel Owners
Claridge Trawlers Ltd.	Vessel Owners
Colne Fishing Co. Ltd.	Parent Company
	Vessel Owners
Dagon Fishing Co. Ltd.	Vessel Owners
Drifter Trawlers Ltd.	Vessel Owners
East Coast Fish Sales Ltd.	Fish Salesman
	Vessel Owners
	Vessel Managers
East Coast Oil Wharves Ltd.	Fuel Distributors
Huxley Fishing Co. Ltd.	Vessel Owners
LBS Engineering Co. Ltd.	Engineers
	Ship Repairers
Lowestoft Ice Co. Ltd.	Ice Suppliers
The Colne Shipping Co. Ltd.	Parent Company
	Vessel Owners
	Vessel Managers

Top Trawler Awards
1987

In 1987, the *St. Christopher* was top trawler with earnings of £845,435. Those in charge of the vessel during that period are seen here with Mr. Claridge in 1988, receiving awards for their part in the achievement. (Left to Right) David Whitlam - Mate who skippered six trips on the vessel, David Athorn - Skipper, Gordon Claridge - Managing Director, Steven Jonas - Skipper.

St. Simon in the Trawl Dock
22nd January 1990

On the 19th January 1990, at sea on board the *St. Simon* with Skipper Tony Jenner in charge, the mast and derricks of the vessel crashed down. They landed across the deck and caused a list to starboard. The *St. Christopher* towed the *St. Simon* home, arriving on the 21st January.

A number of changes have taken place since these photographs were taken. Talisman Trawlers ceased fishing and their offices have been sold, the Fisherman's Mission has been sold and replaced by a much smaller office adjacent to the docks entrance. The well known name of the ship repair firm William Overy & Son is no longer seen at Lowestoft, and the *St. Simon* herself is no longer seen locally, having left the Lowestoft fleet in 1998

St. Croix in the Trawl Dock
1990

A past member of the Colne fleet, the *St Croix* in the Trawl Dock.
The buildings in the background were later demolished. The *St. Croix*
was broken up in 1994.

St. Nicola in the Trawl Dock
1991

A scene gone forever. A view of the Trawl Dock showing the now scrapped Colne beam trawler
St.Nicola and the now demolished fish processing buildings. Apart from being used as a temporary
storage area, no use has been found for the land on which these buildings once stood.

St. John in the Waveney Dock
1991

The *St. John* at rest in the Waveney Dock on the 10th October 1991.
A unit of the present fleet, she is one of the pair of beam trawlers built for the Company in 1987.

P225 St. Lucia

Built in Holland during 1988 as the *Cromer*, the *St.Lucia* joined the Colne fleet in 1994. She is seen here in the Trawl Dock. *St.Lucia* is part of the present Lowestoft fleet.

LT63 St.Nicola

Broken up in 1995-96 at Lowestoft, the *St. Nicola* is seen leaving the port on a fishing trip in the last years of her life. She was built in Holland in 1974 as the *Willem Adriana*.

Colne Trawler Wheelhouse
1995

A view inside the wheelhouse of one of the trawlers built in the late 1980s.

Colne Shipping
1996
The management team of Colne Shipping in 1996
(Left to right) Hugh Sims-Finance Manager and Deputy General Manager,
Ian Colby-Assistant Manager, Bob Hovells-General Manager,
Harry Moore-Superintendent Engineer and Robin Claridge-Managing Director.

Lowestoft

A view of the Fish Processing Hall, Waveney Dock

Trawl Dock
1996

A view showing the Colne vessels *Eta*, *St. Mark* and the *Gordon David*. Both
Eta and *St. Mark* remain in the fleet. The *Gordon David* was sold in 1998.

Trawl Dock
1996

Colne vessels in the Trawl Dock. From left to right are *Gordon David*, *St. Davids*
and furthest from the camera the *St.Vincent*. Only the *St. Davids* remains in the
present fleet, both the *St.Vincent* and *Gordon David* were sold during 1998.

Waveney Dock
1997

The Colne beam trawler *St. Lucia* at a landing berth in the Waveney Dock

Fish Auction

Despite the recent introduction of electronically driven fish auctions at Lowestoft, and the media hype surrounding them, the "shout" auctions continue in 2000. This typical Colne fish selling scene was recorded in 1997.

St. Anthony
1999

The newly arrived *St. Anthony* berthed at the west end of the Trawl Dock.
She arrived at Lowestoft on the afternoon of Saturday, 27th March 1999

St. Anthony
1999

Two views of the wheelhouse shortly after she was delivered

VESSELS OF THE FLEET

ADDITIONS

During the first ten-year period of the Group's existence, all the vessels in the fleet were purchased from other owners. It was to be several years before any new vessel would join the fleet. The first two vessels to be bought by Mr. Gordon Claridge were a steam drifter/trawler and a small diesel powered trawler.
The steam-powered vessel was the Swansea registered *Lass O'Doune*, built in 1910 at Aberdeen for George Falconer and others of Gardenstown. Originally registered at Banff, she ceased fishing in the 1920s when sold to the pilot authorities at Cardiff for use as a pilot vessel. *Lass O'Doune* was retained on this work until 1943 when she was sold to Swansea owners and returned to fishing. Mr. Claridge purchased her in 1945.
The diesel-engined trawler had been built as the experimental forerunner of a class that was expected to revolutionise the Lowestoft trawling fleet.
This vessel was the *Ala*, built in 1933 by Richards Ironworks Ltd. at Lowestoft, to the order of Mr. W. F. Cockrell of the East Anglian Ice and Cold Storage Co. Ltd. A small trawler of about seventy-five feet in length, *Ala* was the first of twelve ordered by Mr. Cockrell for a new Company, LT (1934) Ltd. He hoped that these vessels would lead the way to the modernisation of the Lowestoft trawling fleet. However, the building and experience gained with *Ala*, also substantially helped Grimsby commence modernisation of their trawling fleet. Seven of the twelve had been completed by the beginning of World War II, these being *Ala, Eta, Willa, Gula, Rotha, Rewga,* and *Celita*. The war put a stop to the building programme, and no more were ever built. Mr. Claridge's group of companies later owned all of the class with the exception of *Eta*, which was a war-loss.
Five slightly larger vessels of a very different design were completed in 1949 and 1950, having been built for the Ice Company and for Small & Co. (Lowestoft) Ltd. These companies were closely associated and the five vessels could perhaps, be seen as the post war completion of Mr. Cockrell's original order. These vessels were built as drifter/trawlers, however not all were used for drifting. The *W. F. Cockrell* and *B. R. Banks* were built for the Ice Company and *Frederick Spashett, Henrietta Spashett* and *George Spashett* were built for subsidiary

companies of Small & Co. (Lowestoft) Ltd. The year 1946 saw another of the "Ala" class of vessels added to Mr. Claridge's fleet, when he purchased the *Gula*. Two other vessels were also added in that year, the *Fertile,* an Ayr registered steam drifter/trawler, which had been built at Dundee in 1907, by the Caledon Shipbuilding Company. The other vessel was purchased from the Admiralty, although she had been built as a commercial trawler in 1935. She was the *Guava*, built by Richards at Lowestoft as the *British Columbia* to the order of Grimsby Motor Trawlers Ltd. The chairman of that Company was Mr. J. Carl Ross. *British Columbia* was Grimsby's first North Sea diesel powered trawler, and like the *Ala* was somewhat experimental when built. During World War II she served as a naval vessel, having been purchased by the Admiralty and renamed *Guava* in 1939. Later in 1949, she was to regain her original name.
During 1947 the remaining four "Ala" class vessels, the *Rotha, Rewga, Willa* and *Celita,* came into Colne ownership, and their addition bought the fleet total to nine. However, with the sale of *Ala* and the loss of the *Lass O'Doune,* the fleet at the end of that year had been reduced to seven. The following year saw the first purchase of several 90 foot Motor Fishing Vessels (MFVs) which the Admiralty had just commenced selling.
During the war, the Admiralty took over large numbers of drifters and trawlers for use as harbour service, patrol and examination and anti-submarine vessels, minesweepers and other uses. Many of these vessels were lost, and to replace them, the Admiralty designed types of vessels which would not only serve their wartime requirements, but would be suitable for use by the fishing industry after the war was over. The two bought in 1948 were *MFV1506*, built in 1944 by Richards at Lowestoft, and *MFV1542*. Mr. Claridge gave the names of *Eta* to *1506,* and *Ala* to *1542*. The first vessel to be named *Ala* had by then left the fleet having been sold the previous year. These MFVs were powered originally by 240hp Crossley diesel engines; later some were re-engined with units that were more powerful.
During 1949, several additions were made to the fleet. Another former Admiralty vessel was purchased, this time it was a motor minesweeper built at Pembroke Dock in 1945. The original *Guava* had by now been renamed *British Columbia* and this gave an opportunity for the latest addition to be named *Guava*. Only a small number of vessels of this type joined the British fishing fleet, those that did operated from Aberdeen. However, several served in fleets on the Continent. Another 90 foot MFV, the *Kristin* was purchased, this vessel came from Oddsons

Ltd. of Hull. She was later re-registered at Lowestoft as *LT68,* and in 1952 briefly became the *Albercore,* before becoming the *Albacore.*

That year also saw the purchase from the Milford Steam Trawling Co. Ltd., of their trawler *Milford Knight (M176).* The purchase of this vessel started a trend, which was rather unusual. All the diesel powered vessels ever owned by the Milford Steam Trawling Co. Ltd., with the exception of the *Milford Viscount* which was lost, were to come, either directly or indirectly, into the ownership of the Colne group of companies. This *Milford Knight* had been built at Selby on the Humber, by Cochrane & Sons Ltd. in 1936 for Grimsby Motor Trawlers Ltd., the design being based on the *British Columbia.* She was named *British Guiana* and worked from Grimsby until being taken over by the Navy at the beginning of the war. After the end of the war she was bought by Mr. F. E. Catchpole of Lowestoft, who renamed her *Sunlit Waters.* She was however, considered at that time to be too big to work from Lowestoft, and was sold to south west interests in Brixham. By 1947, she had been sold to Milford, becoming *Milford Knight.*

The next year, 1950, saw only one vessel added to the Colne fleet, this was the sister ship of the *Milford Knight,* a vessel named *Milford Baron.* Cochrane at Selby had built her in 1937 for Grimsby Motor Trawlers Ltd., as the *British Honduras.* After war service, she also came to Lowestoft, becoming *Peaceful Star* in the Star Drift Company's fleet. However, like *Sunlit Waters* she was considered too big for Lowestoft and went to the West Coast. Both *Milford Knight* and *Milford Baron* reverted to their pre-war names of *British Guiana* and *British Honduras* after joining the Colne fleet.

Festival of Britain year, 1951, saw three more of the 90 foot MFV class added to the Colne fleet, by the purchase of the Huxley Fishing Co. Ltd. of Grimsby. This concern had been associated with H. Markham Cook and with Northern Trawlers Ltd. The three MFVs which changed hands with the Company were the *Aylesby* (which was another product of Richards Ironworks Ltd. of Lowestoft), *Enderby* and *Grasby.* The last named had already been working from the port, under management, for some time. *Aylesby* was unfortunately lost at sea, by fire, not long after she commenced operations at the port for her new owners.

The following year was to see several vessels added to the fleet. These were three more 90-foot MFVs, a similar commercially built drifter/trawler, a 75-foot drifter acquired with another Company, and two steam drifter/trawlers. Although purchased mainly for scrapping in connection with the WFA's "scrap and built" loan scheme, the steam-powered vessels did fish for a number of years. The MFVs were the *Alorburn* and *Maravanne* both from Aberdeen owners, and the *Sea Monarch* from Milford Haven owners. *Sea Monarch* became the *Red Snapper* in 1952, and in 1953 was renamed the *Snapper.* The diesel powered drifter/trawler was the Peterhead registered *Equity I.* She was of similar design to the ex-Admiralty vessels, but had been built by Brooke Marine Ltd. at Oulton

Broad in 1948. She became the *Madame Prunier* in 1953. Her previous owners had been the Scottish Co-operative Wholesale Society. The 75-foot drifter, which never came to Lowestoft, but did fish from Great Yarmouth, was the Aberdeen registered *Cedargrove.* The Clan Steam Fishing Co. Ltd. and others, possibly including the skipper, had jointly owned this vessel. The two steam vessels were *Buckler,* which had been built at Great Yarmouth in 1911, and had always been owned at Lowestoft, and the *Flora Taylor.* Built by J. W. Brooke Ltd., at Oulton Broad in 1919 as *Moonset,* she was one of the numerous Admiralty standard drifters. Bought by the Scottish Fishery Board in 1920, she became the Peterhead registered *Flora Taylor.* Later owned by Irvin of Shields, she was sold in 1930 and registered at Lowestoft.

During the next two years, 1953 and 1954, only three more vessels were added to the Colne fleet, these all being steam powered drifter/trawlers, the *Calm Waters, Vera Creina* and *Patria. Calm Waters,* which was bought from Mr. F. E. Catchpole in 1953 was another standard drifter, built at Hook in 1918 by the Ouse Shipbuilding Co. Ltd. as the *Dew.* She had a variety of owners, names and registrations before becoming the *Calm Waters* in 1949. The *Vera Creina,* which had been built at Yarmouth in 1911 by Crabtree & Co. had, like the *Buckler,* always been owned at Lowestoft and in recent years had been managed by East Coast Fish Sales Ltd.

Bought in 1954, *Patria* was a Dutch built steam drifter/trawler, dating from 1916. She was one of a number of Dutch drifters purchased by English interests at Lowestoft in 1930. Before her sale to Colne in 1954, the Shoals Fishing Co. Ltd. one of the subsidiaries of Small & Co. (Lowestoft) Ltd. owned her.

MODIFICATIONS, DISPOSALS, AND LOSSES

The year 1946 witnessed the loss of the *Lass O'Doune,* off the south coast whilst on passage from the west coast. During 1947, the first *Ala* was sold to the Indian Government who used her as a fishery research vessel. She was later sold to the Government of Pakistan. The *Aylesby* was lost in the North Sea, after catching fire whilst on a fishing trip during 1951, and her sister ship, *Enderby* was sold to Norwegian interests in 1952.

At the end of January 1953, during the weekend of the great flood, the *Guava (LT73)* was lost, presumably overwhelmed, in the Cap Gris Nez area.

During the same year, the *Equity I,* by now renamed *Madame Prunier,* was disposed of to another Lowestoft fishing company. This interesting drifter/trawler was built locally by Brooke Marine Ltd. She was mainly of wooden construction, the frames, planking and beams all being of English oak with Oregon pine deck planking over 2ins thick. The casing of the engine-room and the funnel, with parts of the wheelhouse, were of aluminium alloy. The fish hold situated forward had a capacity of 4340 cubic feet, and was fitted with shelves and boards arranged for drifting and trawling. Her main engine was a 265hp Crossley two stroke direct reversing diesel, driving a three bladed propeller at 300rpm giving a design speed of 9 knots. The engine drove the trawl winch by a belt and pulleys. The auxiliary machinery of the *Equity I* was a single cylinder 9hp diesel driving a 3.5kw generator and general service pump. Another 20hp engine drove the air compressor. The vessel was equipped with a 15-foot lifeboat. The *Madame Prunier* was one of the relatively few vessels owned by the Colne group of companies, built at Lowestoft or Oulton Broad.

The following year, 1954, saw the end of steam fishing in the fleet, when the steam drifter/trawlers in the fleet, *Calm Waters, Patria, Fertile, Flora Taylor, Buckler* and *Vera Creina* all went to scrap. Their scrapping however, played a vital role in the rebuilding of the Lowestoft fleet over the next few years, as new vessels joined the fleet under the "scrap and build" scheme.
Major alterations carried out to vessels during this ten year period included new raked stems, with foc'sle heads, added to three of the "Ala" class vessels - *Willa, Rewga* and *Celita.* Brooke Marine at Oulton Broad carried out the work.

SECTION TWO
1955-1964

ADDITIONS

The first decade from 1945 to 1955 showed the start and early growth of the Group, and its consolidation by the purchasing of second hand vessels. The next ten years were to see a number of new vessels being ordered. Other second hand vessels were acquired during this period and others were sold or sent to the shipbreakers. Some of the new vessels were built in conjunction with the White Fish Authority's "Scrap and Built" scheme. Under this scheme if two vessels were scrapped a new one could be built with a generous WFA grant.

Orders for the first of the newly built vessels to join the fleet during the second ten years of the Group's existence were placed with shipbuilders during 1953 and 1954. However, none of these vessels was to enter service until 1955.
The first launch for the Company was that of the *Bermuda* at the Selby shipyard of Cochrane & Sons Ltd. This well-known firm of trawler builders had built in 1954 two similar vessels, the *Wroxham Queen* and *Ludham Queen* for Talisman Trawlers Ltd. *Bermuda* was launched on 27th November 1954. She was built to the order of one of the subsidiaries of the Colne Group, namely Claridge Trawlers Ltd, and Mrs. G. D. Claridge, wife of the managing director, performed the launching ceremony. After running trials off the mouth of the Humber,

Bermuda arrived at Lowestoft in May 1955 and left on her first trip to the fishing grounds a few days later.
On the 13th December 1954, Cochranes launched a second vessel to this design, the *Grenada,* for the Dagon Fishing Co. Ltd., another Colne subsidiary. On this occasion the launching ceremony was performed by Mrs. D. A. Stephens, wife of the owner's general manager. *Grenada* arrived at Lowestoft on the 23rd July 1955. Cochranes were to build two more vessels to this design in 1959 and two other yards were to build two vessels each, to the same basic design, but more about these will be found below.

On the 15th April 1955, the first of a smaller class, known as the "Fish" class was launched from the Thorne yard of Richard Dunston Ltd. This trawler was the *Kingfish,* ordered for Claridge Trawlers Ltd. The following account of the launch of this vessel appeared in the " Fishing News " of 22nd. April 1955: -
"A diesel trawler was launched at the Thorne shipyard of Richard Dunston Ltd., on Friday 15th. April. Miss M. T. Shields performed the naming ceremony on behalf of the owners Claridge Trawlers Ltd., of Lowestoft. The *Kingfish* has dimensions of 93ft.B.P. x 21ft 3ins. moulded breadth x 10ft moulded depth. and is of modern design and appearance. Accommodation of a high standard is arranged for the crew, who are berthed aft. The skipper's accommodation is arranged below the wheelhouse.
Propelling Machinery is by Ruston and Hornsby and develops 280shp and is fitted with a 3:1 oil operated reverse reduction gearbox".

The *Kingfish* was handed over so as to arrive at Lowestoft on 27th August 1955 and a repeat order was placed for two identical vessels, which joined the fleet in 1956. These were *Spearfish*, which was launched on 19th December 1955, followed by *Rockfish*, which went down the slipways on 29th June 1956. Five more vessels, of a slightly amended design were to be built at the Thorne yard. The next vessels to be built for the fleet arrived in 1957, and were two of a very similar design to the "Bermuda" class. These were built by Richard Dunston Ltd. but this time at the Haven Yard (Henry Scarr Ltd.) at Hessle. The first of this pair into the water was the *Bahama,* which was launched on the 15th June 1957. A sister ship, the *Antigua* was launched on 30th August 1957. Both vessels landed their first catches during the autumn of 1957. They both had Ruston 446hp engines. Unusually for vessels built at that time for the Group, this pair had black hulls for many years, being repainted grey in the early seventies.
The following year, 1958, saw *Barbados* and *Dominica* arrive from the Grimsby shipyard of J. S. Doig Ltd. These were very much like the *Bahama* in design, although as in the case of the previous pair built at Hessle, there were individual touches that indicted which yard had built them. Like the *Bermuda* and *Grenada,* the *Barbados* and her sister ship were powered by 403hp Ruston diesels.
Cochranes at Selby built two more "Bermuda" class vessels; however, the design

was very slightly altered from the first pair, by adding a foot to the beam. The *Anguilla* was launched on the 16th August 1958, with *Montserrat* following her into the water on the 29th September of that year. They were not completed until the following year. Like others before them, they were powered with Ruston 403hp diesels.

During 1958, it was decided that as a result of two years experience with the first three, to expand the "Fish" class and an order for two more was placed with Richard Dunston Ltd. These were like the previous vessels of their class and built at Dunston's Thorne yard.

These later vessels, the *Cuttlefish* and *Sawfish*, had a lower foc'sle head and a more conventional shape of stern. They were both powered by 360hp Ruston diesels. *Cuttlefish* was launched on 27th September 1958 and *Sawfish* in December of that year, both entered service during 1959.

No new vessels joined the fleet in 1960, but during 1961, five new vessels arrived from Richard Dunston Ltd. Three of these were new "Fish" class trawlers, *Grayfish, Anglerfish* and *Silverfish* and, like their predecessors, they were built at Dunston's Thorne yard. Of these three, the *Anglerfish* had been launched on "spec" and purchased by Colne whilst building. *Grayfish* and *Silverfish* were powered by 410hp Rustons, whilst *Anglerfish* had a 360hp Ruston diesel, like the earlier vessels of this class. *Grayfish* landed her maiden catch at Lowestoft on 13th April 1961, followed by *Anglerfish* on 14th. May and *Silverfish* on 13th July.

The other two new vessels ordered from Richard Dunston were built at the former Henry Scarr yard at Hessle. These two, the *St. Lucia* and the *St. Martin*, had the most powerful engines in the Colne fleet when they were built, being powered with 845hp Ruston diesels. *St.Lucia,* landed her first trip at Lowestoft on 8th July 1961, and the *St. Martin,* brought her maiden catch into Lowestoft on the 24th August 1961. These vessels were the last to be built for the fleet until *St. John* and *St. Thomas* were completed in 1969.

There were several vessels purchased from other owners during the ten years from 1955 to 1964. During 1955, the *Milford Countess* and the *Milford Knight* were purchased from the fleet of the Milford Steam Trawling Co. Ltd. Cochranes had built these two vessels at Selby in 1950, to the order of the Milford concern. *Milford Countess* was the first to sail round from the west, arriving at Lowestoft on 12th. March 1955 and landing her first trip from the North Sea grounds later in that month. She was later renamed *Tobago. Milford Knight* arrived at Lowestoft later in 1955 and after being renamed *Trinidad,* she undertook an experimental voyage to the Faroes grounds in 1956. Although good fish was found on this trip, the trade did not feel that it had a market for Faroe fish and the idea of having one Faroe trip landed at Lowestoft each week, was not pursued. Another experiment with Faroes fish was carried out some years later, but with a different vessel. The propelling machinery for both the *Trinidad* and the *Tobago* was 420hp Ruston diesels. The next vessels to join the fleet were two steam drifter/trawlers, acquired when their owners, Drifter Trawlers Ltd. of Milford Haven were taken over in 1957. These were *Lady Luck* and *Mill O' Buckie,* which like most of the vessels owned by that Company, were registered at Ramsgate.

In 1958, the Group acquired a vessel that had been managed by East Coast for several years. This was the small drifter/trawler *Togo,* which had been built in 1905 at Great Yarmouth, and was owned by the Jubilee Fishing Company of Lowestoft. Converted to diesel power from steam in 1935, (the Silver Jubilee year of the reign of King George V), for the newly formed Jubilee Fishing Co., she was fitted with a 200hp Mirrlees diesel. The conversion was carried out by LBS Engineering Co. Ltd. and was the first of many steam to diesel conversions to be carried out by that Company. Whilst her diesel was being built, the man who would sail in her as Chief Engineer for many years, was at the Mirrlees factory to see the manufacture of the engine. This enabled him to know his engine thoroughly and she did not miss many days fishing due to engine trouble.

The year 1960 was to see further second hand vessels added to the Colne fleet. Three drifter/trawlers were purchased from Talisman Trawlers, the *Waveney Queen* built in 1950, *Bentley Queen* built the following year and *Underley Queen* built in 1952. Richard Dunston Ltd. had built all three at Scarr's shipyard at Hessle, together with two sister ships; Talisman's *Gypsy Queen* and Boston's *St.Luke,* both built in 1950. These vessels were of an all welded construction. *Waveney Queen* was renamed *Una, Bentley Queen* became *Ira,* and *Underley Queen* the *Unda.* These names brought them into line with some of the smaller vessels of the Colne fleet, whose names ended in "A". All three were fitted with 6cyl 230hp Mirrless diesels.

Another 1960 addition to the fleet was a vessel which when purchased, became the largest in the Group's ownership. This was the *Star of Scotland,* bought late in 1959 from the Walker Steam Fishing Company of Aberdeen. *Star of Scotland* was built in 1947 by Hall Russell Ltd. of Aberdeen and was the first diesel powered trawler built for that port. She had paved the way for the gradual modernisation of the Aberdeen fleet. Her first trips under her new colours were following in the wake of the *Trinidad* some years earlier, by going to the Faroe grounds. Unlike *Trinidad* however, *Jamaica* as the vessel had been renamed, landed her Faroe trips at Grimsby instead of at Lowestoft. After these few initial trips, however, she soon transferred to North Sea fishing.

Three of the vessels bought second hand during 1960 were of an unorthadox design. These were bought from the Irish Sea Fisheries Board and were of German origin. All three had been built for German owners at Bremerhaven in 1948 and 1949 and were later sold to the Irish Sea Fisheries Board, becoming *Loch Laoi, Loch Lein,* and *Loch Lorgan.* In 1964, the Colne Group purchased another former Milford Steam Trawling vessel, when they bought the *Postboy* from the Pronk concern at Ymuiden. Built in 1941 by Cochrane at Selby, to the order of Grimsby Motor Trawlers as the *Le Royal,* she was taken over by the Admiralty whilst fitting out, and was completed as the *HMT Postboy.* During the war the Grimsby concern sold her to the Milford Steam Trawling Company and when she was "demobbed" she went to her new owners and was renamed *Milford Marquis.* In 1952 she was sold to Pronks and became *Postboy* again. After her sale to the Colne Group she was renamed *St.Kitts,* and in 1965 was the top trawler at Lowestoft with a £61,209 grossing for the year, a port record at the time. Two more vessels, the *Thorina* and the *Allan Water,* were purchased from the same Dutch concern in 1964; both were also former British trawlers. The *Thorina* towed the *Allan Water,* her sister ship, from Holland. *Thorina* started fishing from Lowestoft almost straight away. The *Allan Water* however, was laid up pending the arrival of a new engine. The *Thorina,* which was built in 1946 at Beverley by Cook, Welton and Gemmell Ltd. for J. Marr & Sons Ltd., was renamed *St.Georges* shortly after entering service with the Colne Group. When *Allen Water* had been re-engined, she was renamed *St. Davids.* Built a year later than her sister, she was originally owned by St. Andrew's Steam Fishing Co. Ltd. of Hull, a Boston Deep Sea Fisheries subsidiary. Both had been sold to Dutch interests in 1947-48. When built, Ruston engines had powered the two vessels, these were later removed in Holland and when purchased by the Colne Group, both vessels were powered by Deutz diesels. These engines were replaced by Ruston engines at Lowestoft.

MODIFICATIONS, DISPOSALS, AND LOSSES

A number of vessels left the fleet during the decade commencing in 1955. Three MFVs were sold during 1955/6, *Grasby* going to Aberdeen where she became the *Doonie Braes. Ala* was sold to Brixham in 1956 where she joined the fleet of Torbay Trawlers Ltd., and became the *William Allen.* Torbay Trawlers had at that time many 90ft. MFV's in their fleet, like the Colne Group. Also in 1956, the *Eta* was sold to Putford Enterprises, and was later renamed *Arduous.* She worked out of Lowestoft for the remainder of her life. The next two vessels to be disposed of, were the Ramsgate registered steam drifter/trawlers *Lady Luck* and the *Mill O'Buckie* in 1957. Both vessels were scrapped under the WFA "scrap and build" scheme in force at that time. The year 1957 also saw the loss of the *British Columbia.*

An American destroyer which was involved in a NATO exercise ran her down in the North Sea. Fortunately, there was no loss of life.

During 1958, it was decided that the four MFVs remaining in the fleet should be modernised and a local shipyard, Richard Ironworks, undertook this work. *Alorburn* was the first of the quartet to go to Richards for the work to be done. In the Second World War, Richards had been the parent yard for the design of this 90-foot class, and hence knew these vessels well. They had built many examples of these vessels. However, the four Colne vessels to be modernised were built at the shipyards of Frank Curtis in the West Country. The work undertaken by Richards involved the removal of the aft casing, on those vessels that still had them, the removal of the wheelhouse and heightening of the engine room casing. Also included was the addition of a new wheelhouse of modern design with a skipper's cabin aft of the wheelhouse on the bridge deck. Opportunity was taken to remove the original 240hp Crossley diesels and to bring them in line with many other Colne vessels, by installing Ruston 360hp engines. *Alorburn* was, at the same time, renamed *Yellowfin.* She was followed by *Albacore, Maravanne* and *Snapper.* After completion of the modernisation of the *Maravanne,* she was renamed the *Yellowtail.* In the early sixties further modernisation of the vessels of the 1930s "Ala" class was put in hand. The original wheelhouse was removed and replaced with a new one of modern design and those which still had an open bow had whalebacks added. Richards did the work on *Rewga* and *Celita,* whilst Brooke Marine Ltd. handled the work on *Willa, Gula* and *Rotha.*

A unique vessel in the fleet, the Scottish herring drifter *Cedargrove,* was sold to Peterhead in 1960. This Aberdeen registered vessel was well known in East Anglian waters although not at Lowestoft, for many years she visited Great Yarmouth for the autumn herring fishing. After her sale, she became *PD348 Good Tidings. Cedargrove* came into Colne ownership with the purchase of the Clan Steam Fishing Co. (Grimsby) Ltd. in 1952.

The next vessels to be disposed of were two of the modernised MFVs, the *Snapper* and the *Albacore*; these were sold to South African owners in Capetown during 1962.

When the Colne Group bought the *Loch Laoi, Loch Lein* and *Loch Lorgan,* only *Loch Lein* was in her original condition, the other two having received newer wheelhouses, of a modern design. These alterations had taken place whilst in Irish ownership. The Colne Group added whalebacks to both *Loch Laoi* and *Loch Lorgan.* In 1963, the *Loch Lein,* which had spent much of her time based at Fleetwood, was sold to Walter Holmes who was also her skipper at that port. Later she was converted into a stern trawler and taken to New Zealand.

The *Tobago* was sold for scrapping in 1964, after becoming badly damaged whilst running ashore near the North Pier Extension at Lowestoft, on return from a fishing trip. Before she was towed away to Kentish shipbreakers her engine was removed, and in 1973 after having been overhauled, this was installed in the *Antigua.*

The 1905 built *Togo* was also sold for scrap in 1964 but did not suffer the indignity of being towed away to breakers like so many other vessels. In fact, she acted as a tug, and took the engineless hulk of the *Tobago* with her to the breakers.

SECTION THREE
1965-1974

ADDITIONS

During the period 1965-1974, only new two trawlers were built for the Colne Group. These sister ships came from the Richard Dunston shipyard at Hessle, and were the *St. John* and *St. Thomas,* both built in 1969. These vessels had the forward facing style of wheelhouse, which had become so familiar in the fleets of British trawlers during the previous ten years, fitted to them. They became the first in the fleet to be so fitted.

The dimensions of these two vessels were similar to the *St. Lucia* and *St. Martin,* but they were of a more modern design. Their propulsion units were Ruston Paxman 1350hp diesels. The *St. John* landed her maiden trip at Lowestoft on 5th. May 1969 and *St. Thomas* landed on the 28th. July 1969, also at Lowestoft. Two more former Milford Steam Trawling Company vessels were purchased, this time from French owners at Dieppe. These were the *Jean Vauquelin,* formerly the *Milford Duke,* and the *Joli Fructidor,* which had previously carried the name *Milford Duchess.* Both vessels were built at Selby in 1949 by Cochrane & Sons Ltd., based on the design of the *Milford Marquis,* but slightly larger. Like the *Thorina* and the *Allen Water* before them, one arrived at Lowestoft under tow from the other, the *Jean Vauquelin* providing the power on this occasion. *Jean Vauquelin* was renamed *St. Rose* and soon entered service, landing her first catch at Lowestoft on 30th. September 1968. It was some time before her sister ship, by now renamed *St. Nicola,* entered service, as she was re-engined with a 1350hp Ruston unit. It was not until 2nd. January 1971 that she landed her first trip at Lowestoft. *St. Rose* underwent an extended refit, which included re-engining with a similar Ruston engine, in 1973-74.

As with *British Guiana* and *British Honduras* before them, these two ships had their appearance altered by the cutting down and capping of their funnels. *St. Rose* and *St. Nicola* were, at the time, the largest vessels in the Colne fleet.

Until about 1963, the harbour authorities at Lowestoft, firstly the Railway Companies, succeeded by British Rail and later the British Transport Docks Board, had provided tugs for harbour towage. After the sale of the *Lound* and the laying up of the *Ness Point,* they decided not to replace these. The Lowestoft Fishing Vessel Owners Association then bought a small harbour tug, the *Corlea,* to move their member's vessels in harbour between trips. Some time later, various trawler owners decided that it would be better if they had their own tugs for this purpose.

The Boston Group then purchased the small tug *Columbus* for moving their vessels around the port. The Colne Group followed in 1970, by purchasing the tug *Mardyke,* their first non-fishing vessel, from R. E. Trim & Co. Ltd. of Doncaster. R. E. Trim had only recently purchased the tug themselves, from the Port of London Authority. After the *Mardyke* had been working from Lowestoft for some time, another owning firm at the port, Small & Co. (Lowestoft) Ltd., added to the port's tugs by purchasing the *Elmgarth* from the Rea Towing Co. Ltd. She was soon renamed *Barkis.*

Unfortunately, the *Mardyke* had quite a short career at Lowestoft and to replace her the Colne Group bought early in 1974, the tug *Sean Claire.*

This vessel was originally named *Pinegarth,* and was a sister ship to *Elmgarth.* After eight weeks she was renamed *Ala,* thus becoming the third Colne owned vessel to bear that name.

MODIFICATIONS, DISPOSALS AND LOSSES

Vessels that were sold, scrapped or lost during the ten years from 1965 included the *British Honduras,* towed from Lowestoft in 1968 by the *Kingfish,* bound for a shipbreaking yard in Kent. *Kingfish* was under the command of Mr. Henry Blowers. Skipper Blowers had made quite a name for himself by towing trawlers home from the North Sea Grounds, after they had become disabled. The delivery of the *British Honduras* provided yet another towing job for him. Many of his tows from the fishing grounds had been made in very adverse weather conditions. The two vessels left Lowestoft for Sheerness on the 25th July, the *Kingfish* returning a couple of days later. In the November of that year, the *British Guiana* was towed up to Darlings yard at Oulton Broad for breaking up.

For many vessels, the year 1970 saw them laid up adjacent to the now demolished Morton's canning factory in the Inner Harbour. In March of that year, nine vessels, the *Celita, Rewga, Yellowfin, Yellowtail, Ira, Una, Unda, Loch Lein* and *Loch Lorgan* all awaited their fate together. These were all sold either for scrap, or for use on non-fishing purposes.

On the 2nd June 1970 the *Loch Laoi* towed the *Loch Lorgan* away from Lowestoft, both vessels bound for the Hughes Bloclow yard at Blyth for breaking up. Later in 1970, the three former Talisman drifter/trawlers, *Ira, Una,* and *Unda* were sold to the Portsmouth shipbroking firm of Pounds. *Celita* and *Rewga* were taken to Darlings scrapyard at Oulton Broad on the 6th October 1970.

The two remaining MFVs, *Yellowfin* and *Yellowtail* were both sold in 1970. *Yellowfin* was sold to Mr. Robert Rainbird who used her for salvage work off the south west coast. As her engine had been removed and placed in the *Kingfish*, her new owner had another second-hand engine placed in her prior to leaving Lowestoft. *Yellowtail* was sold to Mr. Stanley Gooch who initially used her as a houseboat in the harbour. In later years, this vessel became very much a local celebrity, spending a long time submerged in full view of the road at Oulton Broad, close to the Lock. *Yellowtail* can still be seen in the year 2000, on the south shore of Lake Lothing, where she was put in 1987. Late in 1973 just before Christmas, *Mardyke* went to the assistance of the *Grenada,* which had gone aground on the Corton Sand. The *Grenada* was eventually towed off, but in trying to assist her *Mardyke* had hit the bank at almost low tide and as the tide rose she became almost totally submerged and her crew were taken off. She soon became a total loss.

During the Christmas period of 1973, the 100 Class standby vessel *Grayfish,* a former "Fish" class trawler, ran aground in the Shetland Islands during tremendous gales. She soon became a total loss, with the vessel later breaking into two halves. Whilst the stern half was still upright, the bow section was lying with the keel uppermost.

SECTION FOUR
1975-1999

OVERVIEW

This period saw drastic changes taking place within the Colne group of companies. The movements of a vast number of vessels during this period present a very complex picture. No other similar Company in the British Isles has ever undertaken such a programme of procurement and disposal within such a brief period of time. It was a time of continuous change and was unprecedented in the history of the Company.

The reason for this was twofold. Firstly, a major reorganisation of the trawling fleet occurred which led to the introduction of beam trawling, and the withdrawal from other forms of trawling by the Company.

Secondly, the involvement in the offshore support work had become substantial and continued to grow for several years. Vast numbers of vessels, mainly relatively modern side fishing trawlers (sidewinders), joined the fleet to supplement the existing standby fleet and also replace older vessels. The great majority of these vessels came from Grimsby.

From the late 1980s and early 1990s, the Company reduced its commitment to this work and finally ceased its involvement altogether. A number of the standby vessels in the fleet were sold to other operators, and at the time of writing, some

are still operational. However, the vast majority of the vessels in the standby fleet were sold to shipbreakers.

A few years later in the mid 1990s, the Company announced a programme of decommissioning several of the beam trawlers in the fleet. Many of these trawlers were dismantled for scrap, at Lowestoft; others were sold for reuse. For the reasons outlined, details of the vessels are treated differently in this Section from those in the previous three sections.

ADDITIONS

An addition to the Colne fleet in the last few weeks of 1974 had been the trawler *Suffolk Enterprise,* purchased from Small & Co. (Lowestoft) Ltd. She was built by Vospers of Portsmouth in 1957 for the St. Andrew's Steam Fishing Co. Ltd., one of the subsidiaries of the Boston Group, as the *Boston Vanguard.* In 1962, she was sold to French interests and became the *Imprevu.* During 1965, she was purchased by Small & Co.'s subsidiary Kittiwake Ltd., and became the Lowestoft registered *Suffolk Enterprise.* Early in 1975, after the change in ownership to the Colne Group, she became a Colne " Saint", and was renamed the *St. James.* In the spring of 1975, Colne purchased the 1959 built Aberdeen trawler *Boston Hercules* from the George Craig concern at that port and renamed her the *St. Vincent.* Like the *St. James,* Vospers built this vessel for the Boston Group. She was originally named *Winmarleigh,* and after trials, she visited Lowestoft, to take on fishing gear, before sailing on her maiden trip to the Faroes grounds. Whilst in Boston ownership she was always based at Fleetwood, and later she was renamed *Boston Hercules.* In the early seventies, she was bought together with her sister-ship *Parkroyd,* by the Craig group of companies, who owned them until late 1975. The *Parkroyd* was also purchased by the Colne Group, and arrived at Lowestoft early in 1976. She became the *St. Croix* at her new home port and made her first landing at Lowestoft on the 4th February 1976. The *Parkroyd* was another Vosper product, and initially worked out of Fleetwood with a Grimsby registration. She was sold to Aberdeen and in 1969 gained an Aberdeen registration.

The summer of 1975 saw the purchase from the Heward Fishing Co. Ltd., of the trawler *SSAFA.* Built in 1958 at Goole by the Goole Shipbuilding & Repair Co. for the Boston Group, the vessel was named in honour of the Soldier, Sailors, and Airmen's Families Association. On being re-registered at Lowestoft she retained her name and she was given the registration *LT73,* a well known number in fishing circles, being that of the *Guava* which was lost with all hands in 1953.

A few weeks later a further acquisition was the three remaining vessels of the Peter Sleight fleet at Grimsby. Prior to their sale they had been laid up at Grimsby for some weeks. The three were very similar to the "Bahama" and

"Barbados" classes in the Colne fleet. They were the *Fiskerton, Scampton* and *Waddington* and all were re-registered to Lowestoft. *Fiskerton* was built at the Grimsby yard of J.S.Doig & Sons. Ltd. in 1962, as the *Balmoral* for the Queen Steam Fishing Co. Ltd. Her hull was based on the *Bardados* and *Dominica*, built at the same yard in 1958 for the Colne Group. In 1964, *Balmoral* was sold to Peter Sleight Trawlers Ltd. of Grimsby and renamed *Fiskerton*.
Richard Dunston Ltd. built *Scampton* and *Waddington* at their Hessle yard, the former in 1961 and the latter in 1962. They were based on the hull design of the *Bahama* and *Antigua* and were built for the Peter Sleight concern and fished for them from Grimsby until 1975.

During October 1975 three more vessels were purchased, one of which, the *Jacklyn,* had already been on charter to the Colne concern for some months. When her owners, Mitchell Brothers, ceased trading, Colne bought her. Richards Ironworks had built her in 1962 for Jackora Ltd., a Mitchell Brothers subsidiary. Her early years were spent based at Milford Haven, but she was transferred back to Lowestoft around 1966.
Purchased at the same time as *Jacklyn* were two vessels that had been managed by Mitchell Brothers. These were the *Brave Buccaneer* and *Hawkflight*, both of which were owned by C. V. Eastick Ltd. of Gorleston. The Lowestoft registered *Brave Buccaneer* had been built by Richards Ironworks at Lowestoft in 1961 for the Boston Group as the *Boston Buccaneer,* and was a sister-ship of the *Jacklyn.* She was sold to Easticks in 1973. A Mirrlees National 475hp engine powered *Jacklyn* and both these vessels. The Aberdeen registered *Hawkflight* was built by John Lewis & Sons shipyard at Aberdeen in 1961 for the Hawkstone Fishing Co. Ltd. In 1971, she was sold to Southern Marine Ltd. of Malahide, Co. Dublin, being sold to Easticks in 1973. Application was made at the end of October 1975 to rename the *Brave Buccaneer* the *Exuma* and the *Jacklyn* the *Barbuda.* The Aberdeen registered *Hawkflight* was re-registered at Lowestoft and given the name *Aruba.* These three vessels were renamed in the West Indian tradition of the Colne Company, which started in 1949 when the *Milford Knight* was renamed with her original name of *British Guiana.*
Three legendary Lowestoft fishing vessels came into Colne Group ownership at the end of November 1975. These vessels were all built at Lowestoft or Oulton Broad as steam powered drifter/trawlers. Richards Ironworks at Lowestoft converted them to diesel power, in the late 1950s and early 1960s. Purchased from the Mitchell Brother's subsidiary companies, *Hosanna, Merbreeze* and *Tritonia* were acquired for stripping and scrapping, having been laid up at the North Quay in Lowestoft, for a very long period. They had been the last true drifter/trawlers to fish from Lowestoft.

October 1975 also saw the entry into service of the new stern trawler *St. Patrick.* This was the first of its type in the fleet, and was the first new vessel built for the Group, since the *St.Thomas* was completed in 1969. She was also the first vessel to have been built for the Group by Richards (Shipbuilders) Ltd. and was completed at their Great Yarmouth yard. In 1975, *St. Patrick* was considered a very advanced design for a near or middle water stern trawler. She had her machinery placed well aft, to keep noise well away from the crew's accommodation. A reasonably slow revving Ruston diesel developed 1650hp was chosen as the main engine, both for fuel economy and to reduce vibration. The crew were accommodated in two-berth cabins between decks. All cabins had portholes and there were single cabins for the skipper, the owner and the chief engineer. When not in use the owner's cabin could be used as a sick bay. *St. Patrick* was designed for both pelagic and demersal fishing and could be adapted to work whichever grounds and types of gear fishing conditions demanded. *St. Patrick* was the first Lowestoft trawler to be equipped with sonar. On landing her maiden catch at Lowestoft on 3rd. November 1975, it sold for £15,091 breaking the port record which had been held by the *St. Rose* for about two months. The first kit of fish, plaice in this case, sold traditionally for a charity connected with seamen, made £150.
The *St.Patrick* landed several record-breaking catches, including that under Skipper Besford on 6th October 1977, when her landing of 508 kit sold for £18,717. On the 20th September 1977 she put ashore 565 kit that grossed £21,736 for a 12 day trip, under Skipper Elsom.
A sister-ship, *St.Phillip* was launched from the same Richards yard early in November 1975 and joined the fleet in 1976. Before the building of these two vessels, all of Colne's new building had been carried out by yards on the Humber.

During 1975, a number of side trawlers in the fleet were converted for permanent use as 100 Class standby vessels including the *Anguilla* and *Spearfish*. This procedure was to become very common as more side fishing trawlers ceased fishing and were graded and converted for their future role.

In June 1976, the Company purchased the *Kennedy*, this vessel was previously the Fleetwood registered *Boston Britannia*. She had been renamed whilst in the ownership of Heward Trawlers Ltd. in the late 1960s. The Goole Shipbuilding & Repair Company built *Kennedy* in 1957 at Goole for the Boston Group. On arrival at Lowestoft, the vessel was allocated the fishing registration *LT439*, although her prime use was as a 250 Class standby vessel. She was sister ship to *SSAFA,* already in Colne ownership.
The Grimsby registered trawler *Saxon Venture* arrived at Lowestoft on the 7th February 1976. Built by Richard Dunston at Hessle in 1959, she had many of the features of the vessels built for the Colne Group at the same yard. *Saxon*

Venture was renamed *Tobago*, thus reviving a name previously allocated to the trawler sent for scrapping in 1964, after running aground adjacent to the harbour mouth at Lowestoft.

A number of vessels previously owned by the Boston Deep Sea Fisheries Group joined the Colne fleet between 1976 and 1985. The Fleetwood registered *Boston Crusader,* previously the *Broadwater,* was bought from the Iago Steam Trawling Co., a Boston Deep Sea Fisheries subsidiary, in 1976. She became the 250 Class standby vessel *Jamaica;* a name previously used on a vessel that had been sent to the breakers. Two others to come from the Boston Group in 1976 were the Lowestoft registered *Boston Shackleton* and the Fleetwood registered *Boston Lightning.* Vospers at Portsmouth built the *Boston Shackleton* as the *Haselbech* in 1960. In 1966, *Haselbech* transferred to Lowestoft to fish for the Boston Group, and was soon making record landings under Skipper Ken Morgan. She was later renamed *Boston Shackleton.* Early in 1982, she joined the Colne fleet and became *St. Claude.* This addition brought the number of trawlers built by Vospers in the Colne fleet to four. The others were *St. James, St. Vincent* and the *St. Croix. Boston Lightning* was previously the Aberdeen registered *Admiral Burnett,* and become *St.Luke* in the Colne fleet. Unlike many vessels joining the Lowestoft fleet at this time, both continued their fishing careers and received Lowestoft registrations. Another vessel arriving from the Boston Group in 1976 was the *Boston Tristar;* formerly the London registered *Captain Foley.* Under Colne ownership she became *St. Mark,* and received the registration *LT 327.* Built by John Lewis at Aberdeen in 1960, she joined the ranks of offshore standby vessels after a few years fishing,

Other vessels joining the Colne fleet in 1976 year included *Judaean, Tiberian, Samarian, Thessalonian* and *Olivean.* Four of these vessels had previously been owned by subsidiaries of Sir Thomas Robinson & Sons (Grimsby) Ltd., with the fifth being owned by the parent company. They were all previously registered at Grimsby. The *Tiberian* and *Samarian* were to retain their original names under Colne ownership, but the *Judaean, Thessalonian* and *Olivean* underwent name changes. The *Judaean* was renamed *Abaco,* the *Thessalonian* became *Martinique* and the *Olivean* became *Mustique.* The *Mustique* was allocated the fishing registration *LT392.* The *Tiberian* and the *Samarian* were both given fishing registrations, but in 1977 were converted for use as units in the larger class of standby vessels. These vessels spent only a short time in the Colne fleet, both having left by 1979. The other three vessels were all converted for use on standby duties, and went on to undertake that work for a number of years.

On the 22nd March 1978, the *Corena* arrived to join the Colne fleet. Built for J. Marr & Son by Cochrane at Selby in 1959, she was sold to Ranger Fishing at Aberdeen in 1970. During 1972, *Corena* passed into the ownership of Forward Motor Trawlers, a Marr subsidiary. She was renamed *Trinidad* at Lowestoft, taking the name of the 1950 Cochrane built vessel, sold for scrapping in 1976. During 1978, eleven of the famous Grimsby diesel "footballers" were purchased and came to Lowestoft. These trawlers were previously owned by subsidiaries of Consolidated Fisheries Ltd. They had been built between 1957 and 1962, at the Goole Shipbuilding and Repair yard, to the same basic specification. The names of these vessels were well known within the industry, and these were retained under Colne ownership. It was not long before *Aldershot, Barnsley, Blackburn Rovers, Carlisle, Crystal Palace, Gillingham, Huddersfield Town, Notts Forest, Port Vale, Real Madrid* and *Spurs* became familiar sights at Lowestoft. They were either fishing or in use as 250 North Atlantic Survivor Class standby vessels. The *Real Madrid* spent only a short time at her new home port. After being stripped of valuable components, she left the port bound for the shipbreakers.

Two further vessels, the *Ella Hewett* and the *Robert Hewett,* arrived at Lowestoft during October and November 1978. They were built at Beverley, and had fished out of Fleetwood. Both came from Heward Trawlers, the same owners from whom the *SSAFA* came in 1975, and the *Kennedy* in 1976. After a lapse of many years, the colours of the famous Short Blue fleet were briefly seen at Lowestoft on these vessels. However, it was not long before the colours of the Colne Group replaced these. Under their new owners, both vessels were converted for 300 Hospital Class standby work and renamed, the *Ella Hewett* becoming the *St. Kitts,* and the *Robert Hewett* the *St.Luke.* In both cases, these vessels inherited the names of trawlers that had left the fleet.

By 1979, the Colne fleet consisted of a substantial number of vessels and an additional tug was purchased in the August, to assist the *Ala* with movement work around the port. The new addition was the Grimsby tug *Brenda Fisher,* built in 1955 at the John Harker yard for Grimsby Salvage and Towing Co. Ltd. In September 1979, she was renamed *Eta,* the second vessel to have been owned by the Colne group of companies, and to have carried that name.

The continued growth in offshore work, and the need to buy relatively modern vessels to supplement the standby fleet, saw the Group in 1980 and 1981, purchase three vessels from British United Trawlers. All three originated from the Ross Group. The first to arrive was the *Ross Mallard* on the 14th June 1980. By October she had been stripped down, grit blasted and had her new name of *Bermuda* on the bows. The previous *Bermuda* left Lowestoft on the 29th June 1980, bound for the shipbreakers yard of Romford Steel Supplies. During 1981, the *Ross Curlew* and *Ross Heron* arrived to join the Lowestoft fleet. The *Ross Curlew* was renamed *Anegada* and the *Ross Heron,* after an engine change, became the second *Mustique.* At the time of the arrival of *Ross Heron,* the standby vessel *Mustique* was laid up with engine problems and to replace her the *Ross Heron* was purchased. The first *Mustique* was formerly the Grimsby trawler

Olivean and was sent for scrapping in October 1981. Cochrane at Selby built all of these vessels including the first *Bermuda*.

Several former trawlers were acquired after chartering, from another major British source, George Craig and Sons Ltd. For the majority of their lives, the Ross Group and its associated companies had owned the vessels. A total of seven of these Selby built vessels made Lowestoft their new home port, and all were renamed. The new additions to the fleet were *Ross Kelly (renamed Caicos), Ross Kelvin (Nevis), Ross Kittiwake (Desirade), Ross Cormorant (Dominica), Ross Eagle (Inague)* and *Ross Hawk (Pagona)*. The largest of this group, the *Ross Kelly* and the *Ross Kelvin,* had been lengthened during their lives, and also converted to diesel power, having been built as oil burning steam trawlers. The other trawlers were all members of the well-known "Bird" class.

Of the ten members of the "Bird" class built, seven eventually came into Colne ownership; all had been converted previously for basic standby work by the British United Trawlers Group.

Two large former Hull trawlers arrived at Lowestoft during May 1979. *Arctic Rebel,* formerly the *Starella,* arrived on the 2nd of the month followed by *Arctic Vandal* on the 4th. These vessels were further additions to the standby fleet, and were amongst the largest purchased by the Company. Cook, Welton and Gemmell built the *Starella* in 1960 for the Marr fleet at Hull; she was sold to Boyd Line in 1975. The same builders built the *Vandal,* a near sister to the *Rebel,* for Boyd Line in 1961. Both were renamed under Colne ownership, the *Rebel* becoming the *St. Matthew,* and the *Vandal* the *St.Paul.*

On 15th March of the following year, another former Hull trawler arrived at Lowestoft when the *Lord St. Vincent* sailed in. Formerly owned by Hellyer Bros. of Hull, she was built by Cook, Welton and Gemmell at Beverley in 1962, and was sister ship to *Arctic Vandal.* In the Colne fleet, the *Lord St Vincent* became *St. Anne.* As with all the large former distant water trawlers bought by the Company, she was fitted with a bow thruster and converted into a 300 Class standby vessel. A further three distant water trawlers purchased for conversion were the Grimsby registered *Northern Gift, Northern Reward* and *Lord Jellicoe.* The *Northern Gift* was towed to Lowestoft by the *St.Phillip,* arriving just before Christmas 1980. On the way to her new home port, she broke adrift near *Spurn* lightship. The *Northern Reward* and *Lord Jellicoe* followed in January 1981. All three were built in 1962 by Cook, Welton and Gemmell at Beverley, and were previously owned by Ross Trawlers Ltd. The *Northern Gift* was renamed *St. Davids, Northern Reward* the *St. Elizabeth* and *Lord Jellicoe* became the *St.Louis.* As was common with all vessels in the Colne standby fleet, these vessels were registered at Lowestoft.

At this time, the position of the British fishing industry was becoming very critical; a great many trawlers were sold abroad or scrapped, whilst at ports all around the country others were laid up with an uncertain future. Trawlers were employed in a number of different roles including delivery services, surveying, guard duties and diving support. *St. Georges* left Lowestoft in September 1980 with her registration *LT402,* replaced with the fictitious registration *VA402.* Eon Productions Ltd. of Pinewood Studios had hired her to take a starring role in the James Bond film "For Yours Eyes Only". Although long since scrapped, she is still seen around the world on television and in the cinema, when the film is shown.

The standby vessel *Tippermuir* was purchased in 1980 from Safetyships Ltd. She was originally the Yarmouth drifter/trawler *Ocean Trust,* built in 1957 by Richards at Lowestoft. Her owners Bloomfields Ltd. sold her in 1963, to the Small group of companies. They sold her in 1969, and she headed for Scotland where she became registered *KY379.* In 1976, Safetyships Ltd. purchased *Ocean Trust* and she became the standby vessel *Tippermuir.* Under Colne ownership *Tippermuir* was renamed *Celita,* a name previously given to the trawler built in 1939 and sold by the Company for scrapping in 1970.

One Aberdeen registered former trawler was purchased by Colne during 1982, and arrived in June. This was the 1960 John Lewis built *Clova,* a vessel that had already seen use on standby work off Scotland. The Clova Fishing Co. Ltd., a subsidiary of Wood and Bruce Ltd, and part of British United Trawlers had owned the *Clova.* Later she was owned by George Craig and Sons Ltd., who sold her to Colne Shipping. In the Colne fleet, she became the *Saltrou.*

Another well-known former East Anglian drifter/trawler, the *Ocean Dawn,* returned home in 1984. Built at Lowestoft by Richards for Bloomfields of Great Yarmouth in 1956, she came under Lowestoft ownership in 1963, when purchased by Small & Co. She was sold by them in 1969, and headed for Scotland, after being sold to Mr. John Muir. The *Ocean Dawn* was the last British vessel of this type fishing; she became the standby vessel *Rewga* in 1984, when purchased by Colne. This revived the name previously allocated to the 1937 built trawler, sold by Colne for scrapping in 1972.

A trawler in a somewhat run down condition arrived at Lowestoft under her own power on the 4th March 1984. This was the Aberdeen registered *Burnbanks,* formerly the *Lothian Leader* and also *Midlothian.* Built in 1959 by Livingstone & Co. of Peterhead, Colne Shipping bought her for conversion to a 100 Class standby vessel and renamed her *Culebra.*

Three similar trawlers, the *Boston Kestrel, Boston Phantom,* and *Prince Philip* were purchased from Boston Group subsidiaries in November 1984 after chartering. All three had been Fleetwood registered at sometime during their lives. However, the *Prince Philip* had been a Grimsby registered vessel prior to moving to Lowestoft. The *Boston Kestrel* and *Boston Phantom* were built at the Holmes yard in Beverley and the *Prince Philip* at the Hall Russell yard in Aberdeen. The *Boston Kestrel*, built in 1966, was the last large sidewinder built for Fleetwood. All three had been on charter to the Company since the spring of 1982. They were registered at Lowestoft during December 1984 and received the Colne colours at that time. The Boston Group had converted the *Boston Kestrel* and the *Boston Phantom* for standby work at Lowestoft in 1978. *Prince Philip* was converted for standby work at the Boston's Lowestoft yard in April 1979. All three under their new ownership were renamed; the *Boston Kestrel* became *Colne Kestrel*, *Boston Phantom* the *Colne Phantom* and *Prince Philip* the *Colne Hunter.*

The first beam trawler purchased by Colne arrived at Lowestoft on the 9th March 1984. The vessel was the *Jacob* built at Zaandam in 1974, as the *Soli Deo Gloria.* She was sold in 1980 and renamed *Jacob.* At Lowestoft, the *Jacob* became the *St. Georges*; the name previously allocated to the large side fishing trawler sold for scrapping the previous year.

At about the same time, the Company bought two further vessels for the standby fleet. One was the *London Town;* a London registered trawler built by Cook, Welton and Gemmell in 1960, for the Hewett Fishing Co. Ltd. Colne Shipping gave her the name *Guana.* The other was a trawler that was well known at Lowestoft, but by different names. Built as the 94ft *Boston Viking* for Boston Deep Sea Fisheries at Hessle in 1965, she was sold in 1982 and became *Fraser Viking.* During 1983 she was sold again, and reverted to *Boston Viking* for a short period, before becoming *Bob Read II.* In 1984 she was bought by Colne Shipping and became the *Togo,* a name with long associations with Lowestoft. During the last years of her life, the Colne Group had owned the previous *Togo,* scrapped in 1964. As already mentioned, the 1905 built *Togo* is noted for being an early conversion from steam to diesel power.

One name that has been seen on four different vessels since 1945, all belonging to the Colne group of companies, is that of *Ala.* The fourth and last vessel to carry that name was a tug purchased by Colne Shipping from Grimsby Exchange Ltd., in 1984. Built in 1966 at the John Harker yard in Knottingley, she was previously the *Herbert Crampin.* Prior to her sale, she was in use at Grimsby fish docks.

The success of the beam trawler *St. Georges* brought about a change in policy concerning the fishing methods used by Colne vessels. The Company embarked on a programme of buying beam trawlers and with this decision, came the withdrawal from fishing of the few remaining operational side and stern trawlers. Over the next two years many beam trawlers arrived at Lowestoft and commenced fishing for the Company.

The second beam trawler was purchased in the late spring of 1984 from Ladran Bay Trawlers Ltd. The Brixham registered *Willem Adriana* was built in 1974 for W. Vooys of Katwijk. She became the *St. Nicola* in the Lowestoft fleet. By the end of January 1985, the third beam trawler had arrived at Lowestoft. This vessel, the *Alida,* was the sister ship to the *Willem Adriana,* already fishing for the company. A six cylinder 1200hp Deutz engine powered the *Alida.* This make of engine would in the years ahead, become the standard for the large vessels of the Lowestoft fleet. The *Alida* became the *St. Rose* under Colne ownership. A further beam trawler, the 109ft *Cornelis Jannetje* arrived at Lowestoft on the 20th March 1985. Built in 1974 as the *Stevn Willem* for A.Visser, she was sold to A. de Vries of Urk in 1978 when she became the *Andries de Vries.* Sold again in 1981 to de Vogel of Goedereede, she was renamed *Cornelis Jannetje.* In the Colne Shipping fleet, this vessel became the *St. Simon.*

On the 7th November 1985, the *Johannes Post* arrived to join the fleet. This large beam trawler was built in 1973 at Warten, for F. Kramer of Urk. She was lengthened in 1980 from 111ft 7ins to 124ft 8ins, and her 1300hp Soc Crepelle engine was replaced with a more powerful unit. She completed a number of fishing trips before her name was changed in February 1986, to *St. Vincent.*

Built in 1974 as the *Pieter Jacob* by West Vlaami shipbuilders, the *Dirkje* arrived at her new home port in December 1985. In June 1986 this 113ft. trawler became the *St. Michael* in the Lowestoft fleet. She was a vessel used to having her name changed, this being the fourth name given to her since she was built. Her first owner was C. Haasnot of Katwijk and her last Dutch owner was H. Kramer of Urk. She was originally powered by an eight cylinder 1200hp Anglo Belgium diesel; this was replaced in 1981 by a 1200hp Deutz.

The number of beam trawlers in the Colne fleet continued to increase with the arrival of the Zeebrugge registered *Atlas* also in December 1985. This vessel was built in 1974 at Ostend for H. Van Duyn of Katwijk as the *Maarten,* and on being sold she became the *Atlas.* For her first fishing trip from Lowestoft in February 1986, she retained the name *Atlas,* although by then she had received her new Lowestoft registration of *LT332. Atlas* was finally renamed *St. Croix* on the 10th April 1986. The *Pietertje Elisabeth* was purchased by the Company in June 1986. At the time, she was reported to be the largest and most powerful beam trawler to join the UK fleet. Built in 1975, *Pietertje Elisabeth* was lengthened in 1978 from her original 119 feet to 131 feet. She became the *St. Christopher* under Colne ownership, and went on to become the top Lowestoft trawler in 1987 and 1988.

Other beam trawlers to arrive at Lowestoft during 1986, were the *Albert, Eize Willem Fokke* and *Lenie Adriana.*

The *Albert* arrived on the 18th December of that year. Built in 1974 at Spaardam for A. Romles, she was lengthened from 112 feet to 126 feet in 1983. Her engine was an 1800hp six-cylinder MaK diesel. At Lowestoft the *Albert* was renamed

St. James. The *Eize Willem Fokke* was built in 1975 by Holland Launch NV of Zaandam. She arrived on the 26th March 1986 and became the *St. Andrew* in the Colne fleet during the following month.

Lenie Adriana was a vessel of 112 feet and powered by a six-cylinder MaK engine of 1800hp. Built in 1974 for A.Van Urk as the *Willem Adriana,* she became *Dageraad* in 1979. After her sale to J. Meulmeester in 1982, she became the Arnemuiden registered *Lenie Adriana.* The "Saint" name given to her was *St. Peter.*

During 1987, Colne Shipping took delivery of two new beam trawlers. The *St. John* arrived at Lowestoft during March, when it was stated that she was the first beamer to be built for the UK fishing industry. The *St. Thomas* followed her and arrived in May. The first skippers of both vessels were members of the Jonas family. Built at the Visser shipyard in Den Helder, these two sister ships were the first new beam trawlers built for the Company. Until then, all beam trawlers in the fleet had been obtained from other owners. Powered by eight cylinder 1500hp Deutz engines, they are 120ft in length. Both vessels remain part of the present Colne Shipping fleet.

Another tug joined the Colne fleet early in 1989. This was the *Anglianman,* which for a brief period in 1988 had been the *Clevelandman.* She was built in 1965 by St. Andrews Engineering at Hull as the *Motorman,* for Humber Tugs. Her name was changed to *Eta,* a well-known Colne vessel name, on the 25th February 1989. She remains a unit of the present fleet.

Two additional beam trawlers joined the fleet during 1989 with the *Eben Haezer* arriving in March, followed by the *Elizabeth* in late July. The *Eben Haezer* was built in 1981 at Zaandam and arrived at Lowestoft on the 2nd March. She left on her first fishing trip for her new owners on the 10th May 1989. In the Colne fleet, *Eben Haezer* was allocated the same fishing registration and name, *LT714 St. Claude,* as that previously used for a side-fishing trawler sold for scrapping in 1986. The second to arrive, the *Elizabeth,* was renamed *St. Davids,* and became the third Colne vessel to carry that name. She was built in 1980 at Zaandam for W & J Lokker of Goedereede. The *St. Davids* was re-engined in 1999. Both *St. Claude* and *St. Davids* remain units of the present Colne Shipping fleet.

Many people were surprised to see the return of the two former Colne stern trawlers to Lowestoft in 1989. As the *Kerry Kathleen* and the *Gavina,* Colne Shipping had repurchased them specifically for conversion to high specification standby vessels. Sent to Den Helder, they were refitted as fully equipped standby vessels and regained their original names of *St. Phillip* and *St. Patrick.*

Two Portsmouth registered beam trawlers that had previously visited Lowestoft joined the fleet in 1994. The *North Sea* and the *Cromer* were built at the Maaskant Shipyard in Stellendam, Holland in 1987-1988 for Johnson's Sea Enterprises. Built, equipped and engined for deep water trawling, these trawlers remain part of the present Colne fleet as the *St. Mark* and the *St. Lucia.* They have retained their Portsmouth registry.

A small beam trawler joined the Colne fleet in September 1995 when the 75-foot Padstow registered *Hannah Christine* arrived in Lowestoft. The *Hannah Christine* was built in Holland in 1991 and is powered by a 230hp Caterpillar engine. Her size meant that she was able to operate within the 12-mile UK limit. She was acquired from David Evans of Padstow, with the intention of evaluating whether she and others like her, were suitable for inclusion in the Lowestoft fleet. She was later renamed *Gordon David,* after the founder of the Company.

On the 1st June 1991, *St. Matthew* arrived at Lowestoft. She was the first of a pair of large beam trawlers ordered from the Maskaant shipyard in Holland. Measuring 131 feet, she was claimed to be at the time, the largest British owned beam trawler. *St. Matthew* sailed on her first fishing trip under Skipper Steven Jonas on the 8th June. Her sister ship, the *St.Martin,* arrived at Lowestoft on the 17th November, took on her fishing gear and sailed under Skipper John Jonas on the 21st November. She was back on the 4th December to land 420 kits and grossed £53,147.

The most recent trawler to be built for the Company is the *St. Anthony.* Already a local celebrity, she was built in Poland and completed at Maaskant Shipyard in Holland. She was the first newbuilding for Lowestoft since 1991. *St. Anthony* arrived at Lowestoft late on the afternoon of Saturday 27th March 1999 and local and national dignitaries visited her the following week. Her main engine is a Deutz SBV9M628, her auxiliaries are two Deutz BF6M 1015C diesels and the 120 hp bow thruster is from Jastrum. Technically, she is considered one of the most advanced trawlers in the British fishing industry. She landed her first catch on the 12th April when her first kit of plaice, sold for charity, fetched £1330. Her total catch of 22574 kg from 12 days at sea made £38,103.

A very experienced and well-known skipper, Mr. Ray Reynolds, skippers the *St. Anthony.* Before working for Colne Shipping, he worked for the Lowestoft fishing company of Small & Co. (Lowestoft) Ltd.

At just over 138 feet overall, *St. Anthony* is the largest of the nine trawlers in the Colne Shipping fleet, and one of the largest vessels ever to fish from Lowestoft.

LOSSES AND DISPOSAL OF VESSELS

Because of the great number of vessels disposed of between 1975 and 1999, many as bulk disposals, in this Section only, vessels have been presented wherever possible, in previous ownership groups. e.g. all former Consolidated Fisheries vessels are grouped together. Disposal of the individually purchased vessels is included as a group at the end of the section.

DISPOSAL AND LOSSES OF VESSELS BOUGHT FROM BOSTON DEEP SEA FISHERIES

The Fleetwood registered *Boston Lightning* joined the Lowestoft fleet in December 1976, and became the *St. Luke*. Early in the morning of the 18th May 1978, the *St. Luke* was abandoned by her crew of 11 after an explosion occurred while the nets were being hauled. She was fishing about 160 miles off the Yorkshire Coast. The explosion was thought to have been caused by a mine or similar device. The *St. Luke* was built by Hall Russell as the Aberdeen registered *Admiral Burnett* in 1961. At 391 tons, she was one of Lowestoft's largest trawlers.

The Colne Group also purchased the *Boston Crusader*, another Fleetwood trawler in 1976. Built in 1958 by Goole Shipbuilding and Repair, she was purchased by Drifter Trawlers Ltd., a Colne subsidiary. Conversion to a 250 Class standby vessel took place in late 1976 and early 1977 when she became the *Jamaica*. During December 1986, the *Jamaica* was sold to Liguria Maritime for scrapping.

A well-known Boston Group trawler, the *Haselbech,* was transferred to the Lowestoft Boston fleet in 1966 and renamed *Boston Shackleton.* She soon became known for landing record-breaking catches. During 1982 she was sold to Colne Shipping and renamed *St. Claude.* As such, she left Lowestoft for scrapping at the G T Services yard on the 15th July 1986. She was towed there by the tug *Eugenio. St. Claude* had remained fishing until April 1986.

The standby vessel *St. Mark* sank on the 6th August 1990 after a collision with the tug *Vikingbank* off the north Norfolk coast. She was formerly the Grimsby registered *Boston Tristar* and before that, the London registered *Captain Foley.* The crew took to the liferaft and were picked up by the supply vessel *Suffolk Mariner.* Later they were airlifted to hospital at Gorleston. The tug was towing a barge and apparently escaped damage. The *St. Mark* sank in 85 feet of water. Other vessels were bought from the Boston Group and later sold by Colne to shipbreakers. The *Colne Phantom,* formerly the *Boston Phantom,* headed for the shipbreakers on the 6th January 1992. However, by the 4th April she had been towed back to Lowestoft after being resold. After work had been carried out on her, she left bound for South Africa as the *Colne Phantom* of Kingstown to resume her fishing career. The *Colne Hunter,* formerly *Prince Philip,* was towed away to Sheerness shipbreakers on the 29th July 1991. Built by Hall Russell in 1963, she was put on the disposal list after suffering a major engine failure. *Colne Kestrel,* the last of the three "Colnes" to leave for the shipbreakers left on 23rd January 1992. This vessel was built at Beverley by Charles D. Holmes & Co. Ltd. in 1966 and was previously *Boston Kestrel.*

DISPOSAL OF VESSELS PURCHASED FROM BOYD LINE

One of the distant water trawlers purchased in May 1979 was the *Arctic Rebel.* As a unit of the Colne fleet, she was converted into the 300 Hospital Class standby vessel *St. Matthew.* During November 1986, she left her home port of Lowestoft for the shipbreakers. *St. Matthew* was built as the 606 gross tons *Starella* in 1960 by Cook, Welton and Gemmell at Beverley, for J. Marr & Son. The other distant water trawler purchased from Boyd Line was the *Arctic Vandal,* also built by Cook, Welton and Gemmell, but in 1961. She became the 300 Class Hospital standby vessel *St. Paul,* and was sold in January 1993. *St. Paul* continued in use as a standby vessel under her new owners.

DISPOSAL AND LOSSES OF VESSELS BUILT FOR THE COLNE GROUP OF COMPANIES

The *Bermuda* was towed away from Lowestoft on the 29th June 1980, bound for shipbreakers on the Medway. Cochrane at Selby built *Bermuda* in 1955, for Claridge Trawlers Ltd. She was the first trawler actually built for the Colne group of companies to go to the shipbreakers; all the others sold for scrapping had been purchased from other owners.

After running aground off the north Norfolk coast on the 30th November 1981, the 100 Class standby vessel *Cuttlefish* was declared a total loss. She had been built in 1959 at Thorne by Richard Dunston, and converted for the 100 Class standby role in the mid 1970s.

A trawler that was renamed in the last year of her life, thus releasing her original name for reuse, left Lowestoft for the shipbreakers on the 21st January 1983. The *Dominica* was renamed *Ross Cormorant,* when a decision was made on her future after she suffered major engine damage in April 1982. Her name and that of *Ross Cormorant,* a trawler bought from Grimsby, were switched, and she went to the breakers as *Ross Cormorant.* She was built by J. S. Doig at Grimsby in 1958.

On the 29th June 1983, the *Spearfish* collided with the drilling platform *Penrod 85* which was drilling 17 miles south of St. Catherines Point, Isle of Wight. The vessel became entangled with the rig and was badly damaged. *Spearfish* was towed away from the rig in a partially submerged state, only her bows being visible. As the vessel was a danger to shipping, after consultation, *HMS Tartar* was ordered to sink *Spearfish* at a safe distance from *Penrod 85.* At the time of the incident, the *Spearfish* was on standby duty.

On the 3rd July 1985, the tug *Michel Petersen* left Lowestoft towing the *Barbados* to shipbreakers at Erith. Built by J. S. Doig in 1958 for Claridge

Trawlers, the *Barbados* spent all her life trawling from Lowestoft. The *Barbados* had her engine removed on the 14th May 1985.

Towed away from Lowestoft on the 20th June 1986, by the *Kennedy* bound for the shipbreakers, the *Bahama* broke free off Aldeburgh in Force 7 winds. She went ashore at Aldeburgh becoming holed on steel piling in the process. The *Bahama* was broken up on the beach. She was built in 1957 at the Henry Scarr shipyard in Hessle, and had been on standby work for about 10 years, after a fishing career of 20 years. The *Rockfish* left Lowestoft on the 16th July 1986, bound for the shipbreaking yard of G T Services at Barking. Since November 1969, she had been employed on standby work, having been built in 1956 at Richard Dunstons shipyard at Thorne.

Disposal of the two stern trawlers built for the Company in 1975 took place during the late summer of 1986. These vessels were the first built for the Company outside of the Humber. The first to be delivered was the *St. Patrick*, and under Skipper David Besford, she went on to land a succession of record-breaking catches that broke all grossings. Some of these landings were made at Grimsby, including one in February 1979 of 795 kit that grossed £27,345. Under Skipper Richard Fiske in May 1983, she lifted the grossing record to £34,405. This vessel is also notable in that she took part in the Queen's Silver Jubilee Fleet Review. During the Autumn of 1986 she was sold to J. Marr & Son and became the *Gavina*. The sister ship *St. Phillip* was sold to Riverside Trawlers at Grimsby and left Lowestoft on the 18th September. Both these departures from Lowestoft were short lived, and by 1989 they were under Colne Shipping ownership again.

After ten years as a standby vessel, the former trawler *Antigua* was sold to Southard Trawlers of Milford Haven during November 1986. In 1992, she was sold to the Supreme Fishing Co. Ltd., Belfast. *Antigua* was built in 1957 at Hessle by the Henry Scarr shipyard.

Close examination of a sailing vessel featured in the newspapers in 1998 revealed that it was a former Lowestoft trawler and standby vessel, the *Anguilla*. Built by Cochrane at Selby in 1959 for Clan Steam Fishing, she left Lowestoft in 1986 after being sold to Southard Trawlers Ltd., Milford Haven. During 1992, she was sold to Supreme Fishing Co. Ltd., Belfast. Eventually the *Anguilla* was converted into a sailing vessel based in the Caribbean.

Perhaps the most futuristic looking Colne side fishing trawlers were the *St. John* and *St. Thomas*. These fine vessels were built by Richard Dunston in 1969 at Hessle. They were however, destined to have a relatively short fishing life at Lowestoft before being sold to Anglo Spanish interests in November 1986. Both vessels were sold to Pesca Fisheries Ltd., Milford Haven, with the *St. John* becoming *Pescafish I* and *St. Thomas* becoming *Pescafish II*.

One of the former "Fish" class trawlers to be sold for further use as a fishing vessel was the *Silverfish*. She left Lowestoft on 12th March 1987 for a new lease of life under Spanish ownership. *Silverfish* was built in 1961 and converted to a 100 Class standby vessel in 1977, when she lost her fishing registration of *LT340*. Her new fishing registration allocated in March 1987 was *LT136*.

One of the earlier trawlers built for the Company in 1955 was the *Grenada*. Completed by Cochrane at Selby, she was converted for standby work in the early 1970s, after many years fishing from the port. On the 9th January 1970, she spent a day on Hopton Beach after running aground, and on the 21st December 1973 she ran aground off Corton. The Corton incident resulted in the loss of the tug *Mardyke*. The *Grenada* left for the shipbreakers at Barking in August 1986.

Leaving Lowestoft the same month as the *Grenada*, was the *Kingfish*. She was the first member of the "Fish" class trawlers to be built by Richard Dunston at Thorne, and was completed in 1955. *Kingfish* was re-engined in 1966 when her original 270hp engine was replaced with a 360hp unit removed from the *Yellowfin*. During 1979, she was re-engined again. For half her life, *Kingfish* had been a 100 Class standby vessel. Before making her own final journey, she was used as a tug and took the *British Honduras* to her final resting-place. *Kingfish* finally left for the shipbreakers at Barking on the 14th August 1986

Leaving her home port on the 30th July 1987 was *Montserrat*, towing the *Guana*. Both were heading to join the Anglo Spanish fishing fleet, having been sold to Pesca Fisheries Ltd. Prior to leaving Lowestoft, the *Montserrat* had been allocated the fishing registration *LT376*.

The 94ft *Anglerfish* was sold to Anglo Spanish interests in the autumn of 1987 and left Lowestoft with the fishing registration *LT377*. She had lost her original registration of *LT391* in 1977, when fully converted for 100 Class standby work. Richard Dunston at Thorne completed her for the Colne Group in 1961, having built her with no firm order. A further example of the " Fish" class trawlers, the *Sawfish*, was sold to Pesca Fisheries and left Lowestoft for a new life under Anglo-Spanish ownership on the 12th October 1987 as *LT375*. Her original registration of *LT66* was cancelled when she ceased fishing, and was converted for use as a standby vessel. On the 10th January 1991, the standby vessel *St. Martin* with a crew of eight on board, reported at 1412 hrs that she was in need of immediate assistance, about 80 miles off the Lincolnshire coast. By 1420 hrs, with the vessel in a sinking condition, the crew had taken to their liferaft. The *St. Martin* sank shortly afterwards.

The last vessel to be disposed of, from the substantial number of side fishing trawlers built for the Colne group of companies over many years, was the *St. Lucia* in June 1991. She was sold for scrapping and arrived at the scrapyard of Chequers Iron & Steel on the 5th June 1991. Built in 1961 by Henry Scarr at Hessle, she was the top trawler at Lowestoft in 1964, and had been used on offshore standby duty since 1980.

DISPOSAL OF VESSELS PURCHASED FROM
THE SIR THOMAS ROBINSON GROUP

The five trawlers bought from the Sir Thomas Robinson Group at Grimsby in 1976 were disposed of between 1978 and 1987. The *Tiberian* was sold in 1978 to Small & Co. at Lowestoft, where she became the *Suffolk Maid*. The *Samarian* was sold for scrapping in 1979 after suffering serious engine problems. For the same reason, the *Mustique,* which arrived at Lowestoft in 1977, was withdrawn from service during 1979, and sold for scrapping early in 1982. This vessel had previously been the *Olivean,* and went to the breakers as the *Ross Heron.* In 1984, the *Abaco* suffered a serious fire in the North Sea off the Humber; the fire extensively damaged the vessel. She was towed back to Lowestoft, and in 1985 sold for scrapping. The *Martinique* continued on standby work until being sold for scrapping in late 1986. She left Lowestoft for the shipbreakers yard of Cook Bros. at New Holland on the 22nd January 1987 with the *Tobago.* The *Martinique* was involved in three memorable incidents in the late 1970s and early 1980s. Two were major rescues, the first in 1979 was saving the crew of a sinking trawler and the second was in 1980, when she towed to Great Yarmouth in very bad conditions, a disabled cargo ship. The third incident occurred in 1978 when the *Martinique* was reported for sailing down the wrong shipping lane in the English Channel. This incident was considered extremely dangerous by the relevant authorities. For his actions the skipper was fined £100.

DISPOSAL OF VESSELS BOUGHT FROM
CONSOLIDATED FISHERIES

All the vessels formerly owned by the Consolidated Fisheries Group were sold for scrapping between 1981 and 1991, with the exception of *Blackburn Rovers.* As already stated, the *Real Madrid,* was the first of the "footballers" to be disposed of, and left Lowestoft early in 1981 for the scrapyard after being stripped of all useable components. *Aldershot, Carlisle, Gillingham* and *Port Vale* went to the shipbreakers in 1987. Of these four, *Aldershot* had spent her complete time at Lowestoft on standby duties. The other three had a few years fishing out of Lowestoft, before they too were converted for standby work. Also during August 1987, *Blackburn Rovers* was sold and left her home port bound for Limassol in Cyprus. She was hastily renamed *Giant Fish* before leaving, and the famous "C" on her houseflag was painted out. Further withdrawals from service of the "footballers" were made in 1991. The *Spurs* left Lowestoft on the 12th July 1991 for Thames shipbreakers, followed by *Notts Forest* in September. The final three remaining at Lowestoft, *Barnsley, Crystal Palace* and *Huddersfield Town* were

taken out of service in 1991, and sold for scrapping. They left the port early in 1992.

During their time at Lowestoft, *Barnsley, Blackburn Rovers, Crystal Palace* and *Huddersfield Town* went trawling for two to three years and they were then converted to 250 Class standby duties. As with the *Aldershot,* the *Spurs* was converted for the standby role and spent her complete time at Lowestoft on that work.

DISPOSAL OF VESSELS BOUGHT FROM
C. V. EASTICK

Of the two trawlers purchased from C. V. Eastick Ltd., the *Aruba* had a short spell of fishing as *LT 213* before being converted for 100 Class standby work. The other vessel, *Exuma,* was converted for use as a 100 Class standby vessel shortly after being purchased. The *Exuma* was built at Richards in Lowestoft, and had previously been the Lowestoft registered trawler *Boston Buccaneer* and later the *Brave Buccaneer.* She left for the shipbreakers in January 1992.

The *Aruba* was originally the Aberdeen owned and registered *Hawkflight.* Built by John Lewis in 1961, she had carried two Aberdeen registrations, *A215* and *A530,* during her life, in addition to the Lowestoft fishing registration. She had two other owners before coming into the ownership of the Colne Shipping. *Aruba* left Lowestoft for the shipbreakers on the 8th August 1991

DISPOSAL OF VESSELS BOUGHT FROM
THE GEORGE CRAIG AND SONS GROUP

The trawler *St. Vincent* was towed out of Lowestoft by the tug *Eugenio* on the 19th October 1985. She was bound for the Gravesend shipbreakers yard of Henderson and Morez. She fished out of Fleetwood, Aberdeen and Lowestoft during her life, and in April 1985 was involved in a special navigational project, for which she was painted orange complete with her fishing registration. Previously the Aberdeen registered *Boston Hercules;* she was built as the Fleetwood trawler *Winmarleigh.* The *St. Vincent* came into Colne ownership in March 1975, and was never converted for standby work.

Another of the few trawlers bought by the Company in the 1970s, and never converted for standby work was the *St. Croix.* She fished all her life. Before coming into Colne ownership in 1976, she was the Aberdeen registered *Parkroyd.* When built, she was Grimsby registered but worked out of Fleetwood. During the early part of January 1986, she was stripped in preparation for scrapping. She left Lowestoft bound for the shipbreakers yard of Henderson and Morez on the 27th January 1986, towed by the tug *Diligent.*

Purchased from George Craig in 1982, the standby vessel *Saltrou* was sold to Warbler Shipping for further use as a standby vessel during 1987. Formerly the Aberdeen trawler and standby vessel *Clova,* she was built by John Lewis in 1960. As a unit of the Warbler Shipping fleet, she became the *Dawn Saviour,* and during 1993 was sold to Middle East buyers, and became the *Seaguard.* Withdrawal from service of the former Ross Group vessels purchased from George Craig during 1982, started in 1987. The first withdrawals were the two oldest and largest vessels of the group, the 250 Class *Caicos* and *Nevis* (formerly *Ross Kelly* and *Ross Kelvin*). These left their home port for the shipbreakers during September 1987. Their previous owners had converted both of them for the offshore standby role in 1981, and both were fitted with bow thrusters in 1984 at the Brooke Marine shipyard.

The four former Ross "Bird" class vessels continued with their offshore duties until 1991, when preparations were made for their disposal. During their time with Colne these had all been designated 150 Class vessels. *Desirade, Dominica* and *Pagona* left Lowestoft for shipbreakers yards in the latter half of 1991, followed by *Inagua* in January 1992.

Note

The *Winmarleigh (St.Vincent)* and the *Parkroyd (St.Croix)* were sister ships, as was the *Haselbech (St.Claude)* which is referred to elsewhere. All were built by Vospers of Portsmouth.

DISPOSAL OF VESSELS BOUGHT FROM HEWARD TRAWLERS

The *Kennedy* left Lowestoft on the 20th June 1986, bound for shipbreakers at Barking towing the *Bahama. Kennedy* was built for the Boston Group as the *Boston Britannia*, and was renamed in 1968 after purchase by Heward Trawlers. Colne purchased her in 1976 and retained her name. She commenced 250 Class standby work in August 1976.

After being sold for scrapping, the *SSAFA* left Lowestoft on the 12th July 1987. She was built in 1958 by Goole Shipbuilding and Repair for the Boston Group. *SSAFA* spent some time fishing for the Colne Group, but for the majority of her time, she was employed as a 250 Class standby vessel. As with the *Kennedy*, her name was unchanged under Colne Group ownership.

Disposal of the last two former Heward trawlers was in December 1992 and in March 1993. The first of these to leave the Colne fleet was the *St.Luke*, followed by the *St. Kitts*. Previously the *Robert Hewett* and the *Ella Hewett*, both vessels had been converted into 300 Hospital Class standby vessels. They were both built at Beverley. After their sale, they continued in service as standby vessels.

DISPOSAL OF VESSELS BOUGHT FROM LT (1934) CO. LTD.

Three of the "Ala" class trawlers purchased from LT (1934) Ltd. were disposed of before 1975, and are dealt with in other sections. Details of the disposal of the *Ala* can be found in Section 1, and disposal of the *Celita* and *Rewga* in Section 3. The vessels in the class had a long outstanding career in fishing, and later in offshore support. Substantially altered in the 1950s and 1960s they continued to earn money for their owners, and achieved around 50 years service. The last three vessels of the class, *Willa, Gula* and *Rotha* all went to the shipbreakers in 1986.

On the 27th June, the *Willa*, the third of the "Ala" class to be built, left her home port for the last time bound for the shipbreakers. She was lengthened in the 1950s from 75ft to 82ft, and fished until mid 1971 when she became a basic standby vessel. Built in 1936 by Richards as the fourth of the "Ala" class, the *Gula* left for the shipbreakers on the 4th July. Fishing until mid 1972, she was then converted for the standby role. The fifth of the "Ala" class to be built, the *Rotha* left Lowestoft for the shipbreakers on the 9th July. After war service she was bought by Mr. G. Claridge and fished up to mid 1971, when she also became a standby vessel.

DISPOSAL OF VESSELS BOUGHT FROM MILFORD STEAM TRAWLING CO. LTD

Details of the disposal of the two trawlers purchased direct from Milford Steam Trawling in 1949-50, the *British Guiana* and *British Honduras*, are in Section Three. Of the two trawlers bought in the mid 1950s, the *Tobago,* formerly the *Milford Countess*, was the first to leave in 1964 and has been included in Section Two. Both these sister ships were built by Cochrane at Selby in 1950. The other one of the pair was the *Trinidad;* she arrived at Lowestoft on the 10th October 1955, and was formerly the *Milford Knight.* Fishing for the majority of her life, she had a DOT survey in 1975/6 and shortly afterwards had her engine removed. By May 1976, she was in the process of being scrapped at Oulton Broad.

DISPOSAL OF VESSELS BOUGHT FROM MITCHELL BROTHERS

Disposal of the well-known former steam drifter/trawlers *Hosanna, Merbreeze* and *Tritonia* was swift once Colne personnel had removed any valuable and usable components from them. All three were built locally, the *Merbreeze* at Richards in 1931, and the other two by Chambers in 1930. In 1976, they made their final journeys to shipbreakers in Oulton Broad for breaking up. The

Barbuda was built by Richards of Lowestoft in 1962 as the *Jacklyn* for Jackora Ltd., a Mitchell Bros. subsidiary company. She was one of several built to the same design in the early 1960s at Lowestoft. Many vessels of this type were ordered by the Boston Deep Sea Fisheries Group. She was renamed after being purchased by Colne in 1976. Fishing until 1985, *Barbuda* was then employed on standby duties until being sold for scrapping in 1991.

DISPOSAL OF VESSELS BOUGHT FROM
BUT, THE ROSS GROUP AND ASSOCIATED COMPANIES

The first distant water trawler from the Humber ports to be converted into a 300 Class standby vessel was the *St. Davids*, previously *Northern Gift*. After suffering engine trouble, she was also the first to be sold for scrapping. The *St. Davids* left Lowestoft bound for Liguria Maritime on the 28th September 1987.
Three of the Ross "Bird" class joined the Lowestoft fleet during 1980 and 1981. They were all sold for scrapping in 1991, the *Bermuda* in August, the *Mustique* in September and the *Anegada* in December. One however, the *Bermuda*, was later resold for further use in a non fishing role. This vessel took the name of the earlier *Bermuda*, which was sent to the shipbreakers in 1980.
Disposals of other former BUT trawlers involved three of the 300 Hospital Class standby vessels. The *St. Anne*, *St. Elizabeth* and *St. Louis* were all sold in 1992, and continued to operate as standby vessels under new ownership. At the time of writing (2000), two of these former distant water trawlers are still operational.

DISPOSAL OF VESSELS BOUGHT FROM
PETER SLEIGHT TRAWLERS

The first of the three trawlers purchased from Peter Sleight Trawlers in September 1981, to be disposed of, was the *Fiskerton*. Unusually, she had not been converted for standby work and spent her entire life trawling. She was built by J. S. Doug as the *Balmoral* in 1962, for the Queen Steam Fishing Co. Ltd. In 1964, she was sold to Peter Sleight Trawlers.
Leaving Lowestoft for Thames shipbreakers on the 19th September 1991 was the *Scampton*. She had joined the Colne fleet on the 21st August 1975 and spent over five years fishing, before being converted to a standby vessel. Following the *Scampton* a few weeks later, was her sister ship the *Waddington*. She joined the Colne fleet at the same time as the *Scampton* and spent similar periods on fishing and standby work. Their previous owner had named all three vessels after World War II airfields, and these names had been retained at Lowestoft.

DISPOSAL OF VESSELS BOUGHT FROM
OVERSEAS SOURCES

What was accepted as the first successful diesel powered distant water trawler left Lowestoft on the 29th September 1976 for the shipbreakers. The vessel was the *St. Kitts*, built in 1941 by Cochrane at Selby as the Grimsby registered *Le Royal*. She did not fish until after World War II and then it was for Milford Steam Trawling. She was sold to Holland in 1951. After spending many years under Dutch ownership she was bought by the Colne Group and became *St. Kitts*. In 1975, because of engine trouble, she was towed home to Lowestoft and arrived on the 4th October, whereupon she was laid up. The engine was obsolete and with little chance of being repaired, she was sold for scrap and was towed away from Lowestoft by the *St. Martin*.
One of the two large trawlers bought from Dutch owners in 1964, the *St. Davids* was towed away to a Medway shipbreakers yard on the 24th September 1980. Built in 1947 by Cook, Welton and Gemmell at Beverley she was originally the Hull registered *Allan Water*. Sold in 1948 to Holland by her Hull owners, she was bought by Mr. Claridge in 1964. The Deutz engine fitted during her service in Holland was replaced at Lowestoft with a Ruston. The *St. Davids* became well known for breaking records. In October 1966, under Billy Hitter she was the first Lowestoft trawler to break the £4000 landing barrier. She was also the first to break the £5000 barrier with a landing at Grimsby, again under Billy Hitter.
The other one of the pair bought from Holland in 1964, was the *St. Georges*. She was used in the James Bond film during 1980 and left Lowestoft bound for Gravesend shipbreakers on the 7th June 1984. Bought from N.V. Vissch Onderneming De Vem of Ymuiden in 1964, she was previously the *Thorina*. Built in 1946 for J. Marr & Son Ltd. by Cook, Welton and Gemmell at Beverley, she was sold to Holland in 1947. *Thorina* was originally registered at Hull.

The two large trawlers bought from France in 1968 were sold for scrapping in 1985. Built by Cochrane at Selby in 1949 for the Milford Steam Fishing Co. Ltd. they were sold to France in 1955. The Colne Group bought the *St. Nicola* and the *St. Rose* in 1968. Both were renamed shortly before their final voyage, the *St. Nicola* becoming *Willem Adriana* and the *St. Rose* becoming the *Unda*. The *St. Nicola* was towed to the shipbreakers by the Lowestoft tug *Michel Petersen* on the 24th April 1985, after being laid up since late 1984. Her engine was removed in February 1985 and she became the *Willem Adriana*. This released the name *St. Nicola* for further use on a beam trawler that would be joining the fleet later.
After a life spent fishing, it was intended that the *St. Rose* would go on standby work, and all her trawling gear was removed early in 1985. In March 1985, she was painted orange ready for her new role. However, after becoming *Unda*, she

went to the shipbreakers instead. She left Lowestoft on the 3rd July 1985 towed by the *Michel Petersen.*

Towards the end of 1994, Colne Shipping announced that five of their beam trawlers were to be decommissioned and scrapped. The vessels concerned were the *St. Andrew, St. Christopher, St. Croix, St. James,* and *St. Peter.* In addition, the *St. Georges* and the *St. Michael* would be sold. Between November 1994 and February 1995, the first five were all scrapped at the former Richards shipyard at Lowestoft. The *St. Georges* left the fleet in January 1995 to continue her fishing career, having been sold to W. Stevenson & Sons. Also leaving the fleet, but for future use as a houseboat on the Thames, was *St. Michael.* She left Lowestoft under tow on the 27th February 1994.

Decommissioning of another two former Dutch beam trawlers took place between December 1995 and February 1996. As with the previous five beam trawlers, the *St. Rose* and *St. Nicola* were scrapped at the former Richards shipyard at Lowestoft.

Two further beam trawlers were sold in 1998, reportedly to help to pay for the new large beam trawler *St. Anthony,* which was delivered in 1999. Both vessels were sold outside of the EU, to Panama and Liberia, thus retaining the fishing licences and quotas of both vessels. On the 26th February 1998, the *St. Simon,* formerly the *Cornellis Jannetje,* left Lowestoft after being sold. She initially headed for Holland and was displaying her new name of *San Salvador* when she left. *St. Simon* had been at Lowestoft and owned by Colne Shipping since 1985. Most of her trawling gear had been removed prior to her leaving.

The *St. Vincent,* formerly the *Johannes Post,* left her home port of 13 years on the 27th March 1998 as the *Dorita,* her stated destination being Greece. As with the *St. Simon,* almost all of her beam trawling gear had been removed before departure.

DISPOSAL OF SINGLE VESSELS BOUGHT FROM OTHER OWNERS

The Aberdeen trawler *Star of Scotland* came to Lowestoft in 1959 and was renamed *Jamaica* in the Colne fleet. For a number of years, she was the largest trawler fishing from the port. Later she spent several years as a standby vessel. *Jamaica* left her home port for the last time on the 5th July 1976, bound for the shipbreakers.

When the Aberdeen trawler *Burnbanks* arrived at Lowestoft on the 4th March 1984, it was intended that she would be converted into a standby vessel. She was renamed *Culebra* and work commenced on the conversion. After a considerable amount of work had been carried out, it stopped, and on the 24th April 1985 the *Michel Petersen* towed her to a Gravesend scrapyard. *Culebra* never did undertake any standby work for Colne Shipping.

During 1985, the engine was removed from the tug *Eta* and she was beached on the north shore of Lake Lothing. In the autumn of 1986 demolition commenced, and by the end of November 1986, the *Eta* was no more. Before coming to Lowestoft in 1979, she had spent about 23 years working in and around the Grimsby fish docks, as the Grimsby tug *Brenda Fisher.*

On the 26th January 1986, the Colne Shipping tug *Ala* left Lowestoft Harbour to go to the aid of the tanker *Lynded,* aground on the Holm Sand. For an unknown reason, the *Ala* capsized off the harbour. Attempts to raise the tug by Eurosalve were unsuccessful due to the weather and tide conditions. On the 7th July 1986, the wreck of the *Ala* was blown up. She was previously the *Sean Claire.*

A vessel with an interesting and varied past, which underwent a number of name changes, left the fleet for scrapping at G T Services in August 1986. The *St. James* started her life at Grimsby as the *Boston Vanguard.* She was later sold to French owners who sold her in 1965, to Lowestoft owners. In 1974 she became a unit of the Colne fleet and was given her final name. The *St. James* spent six years fishing until 1980, when conversion for the standby vessel role was carried out. She was the last of the four trawlers built by Vospers of Portsmouth for the Boston Group between 1956 and 1959, all of which eventually became units of the Colne Group.

The second vessel to be named *Trinidad* in the Colne fleet was previously the Fleetwood registered *Corena.* She was sold to Liguria Maritime for scrapping, and left Lowestoft during December 1986.

The two former Bloomfields drifter/trawlers that found their way into Colne Shipping ownership both left the fleet in 1987. *Ocean Dawn* and *Ocean Trust* had been very much part of the East Anglian maritime scene for many years, initially fishing from Yarmouth and later from Lowestoft. In the Colne fleet, these vessels took on the identity of two scrapped 1930s Lowestoft built trawlers, that for many years were vessels of the Colne group of companies, the *Rewga* and *Celita.*

Rewga was originally the Yarmouth drifter/trawler *Ocean Dawn,* built by Richards in 1956. She was sold by Bloomfields in 1963 to an associated company of Small & Co. (Lowestoft) Ltd. During 1969 *Ocean Dawn* was sold to John Muir and she headed for Scotland to work. In 1984, Colne Shipping purchased her, converted her standby work and she became *Rewga.* On the 24th February 1987, the *Rewga* left her home port and birthplace for new ownership in Sweden. She was registered at Vaxholm and in 1988 regained her original name of *Ocean Dawn.* In the late 1990s she was purchased by Mr. J. Robertson and returned to this country. At the time of writing (2000), she is based on the south coast.

Celita was previously the standby vessel *Tippermuir,* and before that the drifter/trawler *Ocean Trust.* Built in 1957 at Richards shipyard in Lowestoft, during her life she was allocated four different fishing registrations, those of *KY379, LT469, YH377,* and *LT379.* The last of these was allocated just before she left for Spanish ownership, on the 30th July 1987. Under her new owners, the *Celita,* by now the *Belton,* was extensively rebuilt.

Also heading out of Lowestoft on the same day for a new life under Spanish ownership, was *Guana,* formerly the London registered trawler *London Town.* Bought with conversion in mind to a 100 Class standby vessel, she left Lowestoft having been allocated the fishing registration *LT378,* towed by the *Montserrat.* Built in 1960 at Beverley, she was previously owned at Milford Haven. Before that, she was owned by a combination of Boston Deep Sea Fisheries and Putford Enterprises, a combination that in the future, would prove to be a major force in the offshore oil and gas support sector.

The second trawler in the Colne fleet to be named *Tobago* was formerly the Grimsby trawler *Saxon Venture.* Built at Hessle in 1959 by Henry Scarr, she was purchased by Colne in 1976. She fished for the first 3 years and was then converted for standby work. On the 22nd January 1987, *Tobago* left Lowestoft on her final voyage to Cook Bros. yard at New Holland. She was accompanied by *Martinique,* formerly *Thessalonian,* making the same last journey.

One of the few former side fishing trawlers, previously owned by the Colne group of companies, to survive into the 21st Century is the *Togo.* She was sold to Dutch interests for charter work, leaving Lowestoft on the 27th November 1991. *Togo* has visited her former home port in recent years. She was built by Richard Dunston in 1965 for the Boston Group as the *Boston Viking.*

At the end of 1992 the sale of the two former stern trawlers, *St. Patrick* and *St.Phillip,* was finalised. These fully equipped standby vessels were sold to their new owners for further use in the offshore standby role. Both are operational at the time of writing (2000).

In 1997, Colne Shipping had two operational tugs, the fourth vessel by the name of *Ala,* formerly the *Herbert Crampin,* and the third Colne vessel with the name *Eta,* formerly the *Anglianman.* With fewer trawlers in the fleet and no longer any involvement in offshore standby work, it was decided to sell the *Ala.* She left the port on 7th March 1997, after being sold to N.O.D. Tugs of Maldon.

Leaving Lowestoft for Shoreham on the 17th December 1998 after being sold, was the *Gordon David*, formerly the *Hannah Christine.* This 75 foot beam trawler was bought in 1995 for evaluation purposes. She was disposed of after the Company decided that she was not consistent with their large vessel policy.

CURRENT SEA GOING FLEET

THE COLNE SHIPPING CO. LTD.
LOWESTOFT

At the beginning of the 21st century, the fleet consists of ten vessels, nine trawlers and the tug.

Vessel Registration	Name
LT60	ST. MATTHEW
LT62	ST. MARTIN
LT87	ST. THOMAS
LT88	ST. JOHN
LT90	ST. DAVIDS
LT714	ST. CLAUDE
LT1005	ST. ANTHONY
P224	ST. MARK
P225	ST. LUCIA
Tug	ETA

Scenes from the 1960s on a Lowestoft trawler
(Left) Outward bound for the fishing grounds.   (Right) Preparing to release the fish from the cod end into the pounds

DETAILS OF VESSELS OPERATED BY THE COLNE GROUP 1945-2000

The following log includes vessels that have been owned or partly owned by companies within the Colne Group. Included are other vessels known to have been operated by the group, and have carried the company colours. The names of the vessels are those that were carried for a substantial period of time. In some cases a vessel will appear more than once, but with a different name. Not included are the vessels that were chartered and did not carry the company colours.

Explanation of abbreviations

BDSF	Boston Deep Sea Fisheries Ltd.	HMT	His Majesty's Trawler
BUT	British United Trawlers	LFVOA	Lowestoft Fishing Vessel Owners Association
EAI&CS	East Anglian Ice & Cold Storage Co. Ltd.	MAFF	Ministry of Agriculture, Fisheries and Food
ECOW	East Coast Oil Wharves Ltd	MMS	Motor Minesweeper
HMD	His Majesty's Drifter	WHSN	West Hartlepool Steam Navigation Co. Ltd
HMS	His Majesty's Ship		

SSV - A generic abbreviation. Includes Safety, Offshore, Hospital, North Atlantic and other classes of standby vessels employed in support of the offshore oil and gas industry.

MFV - Motor Fishing Vessel. Built for the Admiralty during or just after the Second World War. These vessels were later sold out of naval service, with many being converted for use as drifters and trawlers.

Explanation of fishing vessel port distinguishing letter(s) included in the following pages

A	Aberdeen	GO	Goedereede (Holland)	LY	Londonderry (Ireland)
AR	Ayr	GY	Grimsby	M	Milford
ARM	Arnemuiden (Holland)	H	Hull	N	Newry (Ireland)
BF	Banff	IJM	Ymuiden (Holland)	P	Portsmouth
BM	Brixham	INS	Inverness	PD	Peterhead
CTA	Capetown (South Africa)	KW	Katwijk (Holland)	PH	Plymouth
D	Dublin (Ireland)	KY	Kirkcaldy	PW	Padstow
D	Dunkerque (France)	LE	Lemsterland (Holland)	PZ	Penzance
FD	Fleetwood	LK	Lerwick, Shetland	R	Ramsgate
FR	Fraserburgh	LO	London	SA	Swansea
G	Galway (Ireland)	LR	La Rochele (France)	UK	Urk (Holland)
GN	Granton	LT	Lowestoft	YH	Yarmouth (Norfolk)

Explanation of columns

Name	The name carried by the vessel for the majority of the time that she was owned, partly owned, or operated by the Colne Group.
Fishing Registration	The registration consisting of port letters and fishing numbers, as carried by the vessel.
Port of Registry	The port of registration for vessels other than fishing vessels e.g. Tugs and SSVs.
Vessel Type	The vessel as she was built. Where "Trawler" is shown, this is a conventional side-fishing trawler. Beam and stern trawlers are identified in full. Where "Drifter" is shown, this is a fishing vessel that could be used for Seine netting, Long lining and Drift net fishing. A "Drifter/Trawler" was a fishing vessel which after conversion, was able to work as a drifter or trawler
Call Sign	The registered radio call sign
RSS/Official No.	The official number of the vessel.
Gross/Net Tonnage	As recorded in official documentation. Given in imperial units.
Dimensions	As recorded in official documentation. Given in imperial units and rounded to nearest foot.
Construction	The type of material used for the construction of the majority of the vessel
Propulsion/Power Unit	The type of propulsion and main engine information. Due to operational considerations, the type and rating of the engine was subject to change.
Build Date/Location	When and where vessel was built. Except for vessels built outside of the UK, the build location includes the actual builder whenever possible.
History	Highlights of the vessel's life, including any change in use. Particular emphasis is placed upon the time when she was a Lowestoft registered or owned vessel. The date given for the selling or transferring of a vessel may be approximate. This information can be subject to commercial confidence.

Name	Vessel Type	Gross Tonnage	Dimensions (ft.)	Propulsion	Build Date	History
Fishing Registration	Call Sign	Net Tonnage	Construction	Power Unit/	Build Location	
Port of Registry	RSS/Official No.			Make	Build Yard	

Abaco	Trawler	291	117 x 25 x 12	Diesel	1960	Built as GY644 Judaean for Sir Thomas Robinson & Sons (GY) Ltd.
	GGHK	91	Steel	5cyl 800hp	Selby	1976 Bought by Colne Fishing Co. Ltd. for use as a SSV.
Lowestoft	301837			British Polar	Cochrane	1976 Arrived Lowestoft on 25th November
						1977 Renamed Abaco in June
						1984 Caught fire on 17th. July in the North Sea. Fire extinguished
						Vessel badly damaged. Towed home
						1985 Sold for scrapping to Henderson and Morez, Gravesend
						1985 Left Lowestoft on 16th November bound for the shipbreakers
Ala	Drifter/Trawler	81	75 x 21 x 10	Diesel	1933	Built for LT (1934) Co. Ltd.
LT347	GDWD	32	Steel	5cyl 150hp	Lowestoft	1945 Sold to G. D. Claridge, Water End, Wheathampstead.
	162963			Ruston	Richards	1948 Sold to the Government of India registered at Bombay
						1968 Vessel regarded as no longer in existence
Ala	MFV	123	89 x 22 x 10	Diesel	1944	Built as MFV1542 for the Admiralty
LT393	GFXS	59	Wood	4cyl 240hp	Wivenhoe	1948 Sold to G. D. Claridge, became LT393 Ala
	166716			Crossley	Rowhedge	1948 Arrived at Lowestoft on 2nd May for conversion
					Ironworks	1949 Transferred to Colne Fishing Co. Ltd.
						1952 Transferred to Huxley Fishing Co. Ltd.
						1952 Reassessed to 92.5ft. x 22ft x 10ft
						1956 Sold to Torbay Trawlers Ltd., registry to BM137.
						1957 Became William Allen
						1957 Sold to John Miller
						1966 Sold to Philip Tree, Gosport
						1982 Vessel reported as being hulked in South Africa
Ala	Tug	62	64 x 19 x 6	Diesel	1961	Built as Pinegarth for Rea Towing Co. Ltd.
			Steel	5cyl 400hp	Northwich	1973 Sold to Swansea owners and became Sean Claire
Lowestoft	301370			Ruston	W. Yarwood	1974 Sold to Colne Fishing Co. Ltd.
						1974 Arrived at Lowestoft on 18th. February
						1974 Renamed Ala during May
						1986 Capsized and sank off Lowestoft on 26th. January
						1986 Wreck blown up on 7th. July
Ala	Tug	44	62 x 18 x 7	Diesel	1966	Built as Herbert Crampin for Grimsby Salvage and Towing Co. Ltd.
			Steel	6cyl 451hp	Knottingley	1984 Bought by Colne Shipping from Grimsby Exchange Ltd.
Lowestoft				Ruston	John Harker	1984 Arrived at Lowestoft on the 8th. November
						1987 Renamed Ala in November
						1997 Sold to N.O.D. Tugs and left Lowestoft on 7th. March

| Name | Vessel Type | Gross Tonnage | Dimensions (ft.) | Propulsion | Build Date | History |
| Fishing Registration | Call Sign | Net Tonnage | Construction | Power Unit/ | Build Location | |
Port of Registry	RSS/Official No.			Make	Build Yard	
Albacore	MFV	113	87 x 22 x 8	Diesel	1943	Built as MFV1516 for the Admiralty
LT68	MRRN	58	Wood	4cyl 240hp	Totnes	1947 Sold to Oddsson & Co. Ltd., became H453 Kristin
	181319			Crossley	Frank Curtis	1949 Sold to G.D.Claridge, registered as LT68
						1949 Transferred to Claridge Trawlers Ltd.
						1952 Renamed Albercore. Re-engined with a 6cyl 360hp Ruston
						1953 Renamed Albacore
						1960 Extensively modernised by Richards Ironworks Ltd.
						1962 Sold to South Africa and became CTA113. Sailed 5th. May.
						1966 Sold to Houmeed Viskbedryf (Edms)
						1975 Sank at Capetown on 26th June
						1975 Raised and then scuttled in July
Aldershot	Trawler	427	139 x 28 x 12	Diesel	1959	Built as GY612 Aldershot for Wendover Fishing Co. (Grimsby) Ltd
	GDYH	139	Steel	8cyl 1120hp	Goole	1978 Bought by Dagon Fishing Co. Ltd., Luton
Lowestoft	301818			Mirrlees	Goole	1978 Arrived at Lowestoft on 3rd July
					Shipbuilding	1978 Converted for use as a SSV
					& Repair	1986 Sold for scrapping in December to Liguria Maritime
						1987 Left Lowestoft on 5th January bound for the shipbreakers
Alorburn	MFV	119	92 x 22 x 10	Diesel	1945	Built as MFV1530 for the Admiralty
LT282	MAWZ	43	Wood	4cyl 240hp	Par	1948 Bought by Northern (Fishing) Ltd., became A614 Alorburn
	182019			Crossley	Frank Curtis	1952 Sold to Clan Steam Fishing Co. (Grimsby) Ltd.
						1952 Registered as LT282
						1957-58 Extensively modernised by Richard Ironworks
						1957-58 Re-engined with a 6cyl 360hp Ruston. Renamed Yellowfin
						1967 Engine removed and installed in Kingfish
						1968 Advertised for sale without engine or gearbox
						1970 Sold to R. Rainbird, used engine installed from Charger.
						1971 Left Lowestoft on 25th February
Anegada	Trawler	288	110 x 25 x 12	Diesel	1962	Built as GY492 Ross Curlew for Ross Trawlers Ltd.
	GHZG	92	Steel	6cyl 785hp	Selby	1970 Transferred to Goweroak Ltd.
Lowestoft	303293			Ruston	Cochrane	1980 Converted for use as a SSV
						1981 Bought by Colne Fishing Co. Ltd
						1981 Arrived at Lowestoft on 27th July
						1981 Became Anegada during September
						1991 Sold for scrapping
						1991 Left Lowestoft during December for the shipbreakers

| Name | Vessel Type | Gross Tonnage | Dimensions (ft.) | Propulsion | Build Date | History |
| Fishing Registration | Call Sign | Net Tonnage | Construction | Power Unit/ | Build Location | |
Port of Registry	RSS/Official No.			Make	Build Yard	
Anglerfish	Trawler	153	94 x 22 x 8	Diesel	1961	Built for Drifter Trawlers Ltd.
LT391	GHWB	54	Steel	6cyl 360hp	Thorne	1976 Converted for use as a SSV in November
Lowestoft	302399			Ruston	Richard Dunston	1987 Sold to Pesca Fisheries Ltd.
						1987 Left Lowestoft on 12th. October as LT377
Anguilla	Trawler	228	105 x 24 x 10	Diesel	1959	Built for the Clan Steam Fishing Co. (Grimsby) Ltd
LT67	GCKU	81	Steel	6cyl 403hp	Selby	1972 Transferred to Claridge Trawlers Ltd. in August.
Lowestoft	301511			Ruston	Cochrane	1975 Fully converted for use as a SSV in December
						1986 Sold to Southard Trawlers Ltd. Milford Haven
						1992 Sold to Supreme Trawlers Ltd., Belfast
						1998 In service as a sailing vessel in the Caribbean
Antigua	Trawler	204	106 x 23 x 9	Diesel	1957	Built for the Colne Fishing Co. Ltd.
LT150	GXKN	67	Steel	6cyl 446hp	Hessle	1971 In use as a SSV
Lowestoft	187025			Ruston	Richard Dunston	1973 Re-engined with reconditioned 420hp engine from Tobago
						1977 Fully converted for use as a SSV
						1986 Sold for further use in November as a fishing vessel
						1992 Sold to Supreme Trawlers Ltd., Belfast
Aruba	Trawler	174	99 x 22 x 9	Diesel	1961	Built as A530 Hawkflight for Hawkstone Fishing Co. Ltd
LT213	MEGC	65	Steel	5cyl 475hp	Aberdeen	1971 Sold to Southern Marine Ltd. De-registered
Lowestoft	302243			National	John Lewis	1973 Sold to C.V.Eastick Ltd.
						1973 Arrived at Lowestoft on 5th May as A530 (De-registered)
						1973 Registered as A215
						1975 Sold to Huxley Fishing Co. Ltd.
						1975 Painted in Company colours in September
						1976 Became LT213 Aruba in January, later in the year used as a SSV
						1991 Sold for scrapping
						1991 Left Lowestoft for the shipbreakers on 8th August
Aylesby	MFV	111	87 x 22 x 8	Diesel	1946	Built as MFV1579 for the Admiralty
LT232	MBDF	41	Wood	4cyl 240hp	Oulton Broad	1946 Bought by Aldred Fishing Co. Ltd. Became GY329 Aylesby
	166649			Crossley	East Anglian	1948 Sold to Huxley Fishing Co. Ltd.
					Constructors	1951 Registered as LT232.
						1951 Sank after catching fire, crew saved
Bahama	Trawler	204	106 x 23 x 9	Diesel	1957	Built for the Colne Fishing Co. Ltd.
LT142	MXYL	67	Steel	6cyl 446hp	Hessle	1976 Converted for use as a SSV
Lowestoft	187023			Ruston	Richard Dunston	1986 Sold for scrapping to G T Services at Barking
						1986 Left Lowestoft on 20th June for the breakers towed by Kennedy
						1986 Tow parted in force 7 winds and ran aground at Aldeburgh.
						1986 Unable to salvage vessel and scrapped on Aldeburgh beach

Name Fishing Registration Port of Registry	Vessel Type Call Sign RSS/Official No.	Gross Tonnage Net Tonnage	Dimensions (ft.) Construction	Propulsion Power Unit/ Make	Build Date Build Location Build Yard	History
Barbados LT312 Lowestoft	Trawler GBHD 187034	213 71	106 x 23 x 9 Steel	Diesel 6cyl 403hp Ruston	1958 Grimsby J.S.Doig	Built for the Clan Steam Fishing Co. (Grimsby) Ltd. 1972 Transferred to Claridge Trawlers Ltd. in August 1978 Serious engine room 50miles off Flamborough, towed home. 1985 Engine removed during May 1985 Left Lowestoft under tow on 3rd July for the shipbreakers
Barbuda LT434 Lowestoft	Trawler GJMU 303686	162 59	93 x 22 x 10 Steel	Diesel 5cyl 475hp National	1962 Lowestoft Richards	Built as Jacklyn for Jackora Ltd. 1975 Transferred to WFA 1975 Bought by Colne Fishing Co. Ltd. 1976 Became Barbuda in January 1985 Converted for use as a SSV 1991 Sold for scrapping
Barnsley LT551 Lowestoft	Trawler GHGD 301827	441 147	139 x 28 x 12 Steel	Diesel 8cyl 1120hp Mirrlees	1960 Goole Goole Shipbuilding & Repair	Built as GY651 for Rhondda Fishing Co. Ltd. 1978 Bought by Dagon Fishing Co. Ltd. 1978 Arrived at Lowestoft on 22nd July 1978 Registered as LT551 1980 Converted for use as a SSV 1992 Sold for scrapping 1992 Left Lowestoft on 20th January bound for the shipbreakers
Bermuda LT122 Lowestoft	Trawler GTBC 186998	204 70	105 x 23 x 9 Steel	Diesel 6cyl 403hp Ruston	1955 Selby Cochrane	Built for Claridge Trawlers Ltd 1956 Top Trawler under Skipper Newbury with earnings of £33,090 1972 In use as a SSV 1980 Sold for scrapping to Romford Steel 1980 Left Lowestoft on 29th June bound for the shipbreakers
Bermuda Lowestoft	Trawler GJWS 304775	266 92	110 x 25 x 12 Steel	Diesel 6cyl 785hp Ruston	1962 Selby Cochrane	Built as GY699 Ross Mallard for Alsey Steam Trawling Co. Ltd. 1966 Transferred to Ross Trawlers Ltd. 1971 Transferred to G. F. Sleight & Sons Ltd. 1973 Transferred to British United Trawlers (Granton) Ltd. 1977 Transferred to Strathco Fishing Co. Ltd., Aberdeen 1979 Transferred to British United Trawlers (Aberdeen) Ltd. 1980 Sold to Drifter Trawlers Ltd. for use as a SSV 1980 Arrived at Lowestoft on 14th June 1980 Became Bermuda in October 1991 Sold for scrapping to Spearings 1991 Left Lowestoft on 22nd August bound for the shipbreakers 1992 Resold and seen passing Lowestoft on 27th April bound for Hull 1992 Reported in use as a salvage vessel.

Name Fishing Registration Port of Registry	Vessel Type Call Sign RSS/Official No.	Gross Tonnage Net Tonnage	Dimensions (ft.) Construction	Propulsion Power Unit/ Make	Build Date Build Location Build Yard	History
Blackburn Rovers LT306 Lowestoft	Trawler GLCA 304781	439 146	139 x 28 x 12 Steel	Diesel 8cyl 1120hp Mirrlees	1962 Goole Goole Shipbuilding & Repair	Built as GY706 for Wendover Fishing Co. (Grimsby) Ltd. 1978 Bought by Huxley Fishing Co. Ltd. 1978 Arrived at Lowestoft on 25th July 1978 Registered as LT306 1981 Converted for use as a SSV 1987 Sold to Y. & P. Fishing & Shipping, Limassol, Cyprus 1987 Left Lowestoft during August as the Giant Fish
British Columbia LT404	Trawler GLRJ 162901	134 50	101 x 21 x 8 Steel	Diesel 6cyl 310hp Ruston	1935 Lowestoft Richards	Refer to GY272 Guava for history
British Guiana LT52	Trawler GYVW 164419	147 54	101 x 21 x 10 Steel	Diesel 6cyl 360hp Ruston	1936 Selby Cochrane	Built as GY331 British Guiana for Grimsby Motor Trawlers Ltd. 1939 Requisition by Navy. Became FY271 1940 In service on Anti-Submarine duties 1945 Ownership passed to F. E. Catchpole 1946 Returned by Navy in March 1946 Became LT93 Sunlit Waters. 1946 Sold to Torbay Trawlers Ltd. 1946 Transferred to Allen & Cooke (Trawlers) Ltd. 1947 Sold to Milford Steam Trawling Co. Ltd. 1947 Became M176 Milford Knight 1949 Sold to G. D. Claridge. Became LT52 British Guiana 1949 Transferred to Claridge Trawlers Ltd. 1966 In use as a support vessel 1968 Sold for scrapping to T. G. Darling at Oulton Broad
British Honduras LT134	Trawler GCCJ 164434	147 54	101 x 21 x 10 Steel	Diesel 6cyl 390hp Ruston	1937 Selby Cochrane	Built as GY513 British Honduras for Grimsby Motor Trawlers Ltd. 1939 Requisitioned by Navy. Became FY272 1940 In service on Anti-Submarine duties 1945 Ownership passed to Star Drift Fishing Co. Ltd. 1946 Returned by Navy to owner in January 1946 Became LT87 British Honduras 1946 Became LT87 Peaceful Star 1947 Sold to Milford Steam Trawling Co. Ltd. 1947 Became M204 Milford Baron 1950 Sold to G. D. Claridge. Became LT134 British Honduras 1950 Transferred to Claridge Trawlers Ltd. 1966 In use as a support vessel 1968 Sold for scrapping. 1968 Left on 25th July for breakers in Sheerness towed by Kingfish

Name / Fishing Registration / Port of Registry	Vessel Type / Call Sign / RSS/Official No.	Gross Tonnage / Net Tonnage	Dimensions (ft.) / Construction	Propulsion / Power Unit/ Make	Build Date / Build Location / Build Yard	History
Buckler LT756	Drifter/Trawler 130004	81 37	84 x 18 x 9 Steel	Steam 32hp(180ihp) Compound Crabtree	1911 Gt.Yarmouth Crabtree	Built for Jas. C. Cooper 1919 Sold to T. Anderson 1920 Sold to W. Thompson and G.H. Catchpole 1942 Requisitioned by Navy 1943 In service on Harbour Service duties 1945 Returned and sold to B. J. Manning 1952 Sold to G.D.Claridge 1954 Transferred to Colne Fishing Co. Ltd. Sold for scrapping in July 1954 Left on 3rd August for the shipbreakers towed by Patria
Caicos Lowestoft	Trawler GVCQ 184936	469 160	163 x 28 x 14 Steel	Diesel 6cyl 1440hp Ruston	1956 Selby Cochrane	Built as the steam trawler GY6 Kelly for Derwent Trawlers Ltd. 1960 Transferred to Ross Trawlers Ltd. 1961 Transferred to Yorkshire Trawlers Ltd. 1962 Transferred to G. F. Sleight & Sons Ltd. Renamed Ross Kelly 1966/7 Lengthened from 139ft to 163ft, converted to diesel power 1968 Registered GY125 1970 Transferred to Goweroak Ltd. 1979 Transferred to Ross Trawlers Ltd. 1981 Converted for use as a SSV 1981 On charter to Colne Fishing Co. Ltd., renamed Caicos 1982 In the ownership of George Craig and Sons, Aberdeen 1982 Sold to Colne Shipping Co. Ltd. 1982 Arrived at Lowestoft on 9th June 1982 Allocated registration LT125 1987 Sold for scrapping 1987 Left Lowestoft in September for the breakers towing St.Davids
Calm Waters LT407	Drifter/Trawler GJJL 139823	95 41	86 x 18 x 9 Steel	Steam 42hp(270ihp) Triple Pollitt & Wigzell	1918 Hook Ouse Shipbuilding Co.	Built as HMD Dew for the Admiralty 1920 Sold to J. H. Smith, Torry. Became A361 Dew. 1923 Sold to J. Smith, Lossiemouth. Became INS 586 Moyra 1928 Sold to G.Duthie & others. Became FR231 Olive Tree 1938 Sold to Richard Irvin & Sons Ltd. 1940 Requisitioned by Navy. Became FY1946 1941 In use on Anti-Submarine and Patrol duties 1945 Returned and sold to Northern Trawlers Ltd. 1949 Sold to F.E.Catchpole. 1949 Became LT407 Calm Waters 1953 Sold to Claridge Trawlers Ltd. 1954 Transferred to Colne Fishing Co. Ltd. 1954 Sold for scrapping. 1954 Left Lowestoft on 12th November for Belgium shipbreakers

Name Fishing Registration Port of Registry	Vessel Type Call Sign RSS/Official No.	Gross Tonnage Net Tonnage	Dimensions (ft.) Construction	Propulsion Power Unit/ Make	Build Date Build Location Build Yard	History
Carlisle LT389 Lowestoft	Trawler GHTZ 303283	441 147	139 x 28 x 12 Steel	Diesel 8cyl 1120hp Mirrlees	1961 Goole Goole Shipbuilding & Repair	Built as GY681 for Rhondda Fishing Co. Ltd. 1978 Bought by the Colne Fishing Co. Ltd. 1978 Arrived at Lowestoft on 14th December 1979 Registered as LT389 during June 1980 Converted for use as a SSV 1987 Sold for scrapping. 1987 Left Lowestoft on 10th July for the shipbreakers
Cedargrove A57	Drifter GOIJ	 49	75 x 19 Wood	Diesel 206hp Ruston	1947 Buckie Herd & Mackenzie	Built for Distributors Fishing Co. (Aberdeen) 1952 In the part ownership of Clan Steam Fishing Co. (Grimsby) Ltd. 1952 Acquired with Clan Steam Fishing Co. (Grimsby) Ltd. 1950s Recorded as owned by Clan S.F. Co. (Grimsby) Ltd., Lowestoft 1960 Sold to Alexander Flett, Peterhead, registered as PD348 1961 Renamed Good Tidings 1965 Sold to Joseph Simpson and others, registered as LK680
Celita LT236	Drifter/Trawler GDWG 166686	78 35	75 x 21 x 8 Steel	Diesel 3cyl 165hp Ruston	1939 Lowestoft Richards	Built for LT (1934) Ltd. 1946 Sold to Universal Motor Trawlers Ltd. 1947 Sold to G. D. Claridge 1948 Re-engined with 5cyl 225hp Ruston 1949 Transferred to Colne Fishing Co. Ltd. 1953 Transferred to Clan Steam Fishing Co. (Grimsby) Ltd. 1953 Lengthened to 82ft. from 75ft., gross tonnage to 86 Extensively modernised in early 1960s 1970 Sold for scrapping to T. G. Darling, Oulton Broad 1970 Delivered to shipbreakers yard on 6th October

Name Fishing Registration Port of Registry	Vessel Type Call Sign RSS/Official No.	Gross Tonnage Net Tonnage	Dimensions (ft.) Construction	Propulsion Power Unit/ Make	Build Date Build Location Build Yard	History
Celita Lowestoft	Drifter/Trawler GVWT 187913	115 57	91 x 21 x10 Steel	Diesel 6cyl 360hp Ruston	1957 Lowestoft Richards	Built as YH377 Ocean Trust for Bloomfields Ltd., Gt.Yarmouth 1963 Bought by Small & Co. (Lowestoft) Ltd., registered as LT469 1969 Sold to James Muir, Anstruther. 1969 Left Lowestoft bound for Scotland on 13th. September. 1969 Registered as KY379 1973 Sold to Safety Ships Co. Ltd. 1974 Renamed Tippermuir during November 1974 Converted for use as a SSV 1980 Bought by the Colne Fishing Co. Ltd. 1980 Arrived at Lowestoft in June. 1980 Renamed Celita during September. 1987 Sold to Pesca Fisheries 1987 Left Lowestoft as LT379 on 30th. July 1987 Became the Pescafish V. 1990 In service as the SSV Belton (with registration LT379) 1991 In service off Scotland during September as a cable guardship
Colne Hunter Lowestoft	Trawler GMBU 303784	442 148	140 x 29 x 16 Steel	Diesel 6cyl 1145hp Werkspoor (Holmes)	1963 Aberdeen Hall Russell	Built as FD400 Prince Philip for Parbel Smith Ltd. 1968 Registered as GY138 1974 Transferred to BDSF 1979 Transferred to Onward Fishing Co. Ltd. 1979 Arrived at Lowestoft on 25th April for conversion to a SSV 1982 During March chartered by Drifter Trawlers Ltd. 1982 Arrived at Lowestoft on 19th April on contract to Colne 1984 Bought by Colne Shipping Co. Ltd. in November 1986 Renamed Colne Hunter in May 1987 Transferred to Drifter Trawlers Ltd. 1991 Sold for scrapping 1991 Left Lowestoft 29th July for the breakers towed by Mustique
Colne Kestrel Lowestoft	Trawler GRPH 308710	431 170	142 x 29 x 16 Steel	Diesel 6cyl 1145hp Werkspoor (Holmes)	1966 Beverley C. D. Holmes	Built as FD256 Boston Kestrel for Basil A. Parkes 1975 Transferred to BDSF 1978 Arrived at Lowestoft on 26th June for conversion to SSV 1982 During March chartered by ECOW 1984 Bought by Colne Shipping Co. Ltd. 1985 Renamed Colne Kestrel in March 1987 Transferred to ECOW 1992 Sold for scrapping 1992 Left Lowestoft on 23rd January for the shipbreakers

| Name | Vessel Type | Gross Tonnage | Dimensions (ft.) | Propulsion | Build Date | History |
| Fishing Registration | Call Sign | Net Tonnage | Construction | Power Unit/ | Build Location | |
Port of Registry	RSS/Official No.			Make	Build Yard	
Colne Phantom	Trawler	431	142 x 29 x 16	Diesel	1965	Built as FD252 Boston Phantom for the Eton Fishing Co. Ltd.
	GRPU	170	Steel	6cyl 1145hp	Beverley	1974 Transferred to BDSF
Lowestoft	303800			Werkspoor	C .D. Holmes	1978 Arrived at Lowestoft on 7th. December
				(Holmes)		1979 Converted for use as a SSV during January
						1982 Chartered by the Colne group
						1984 Bought by Colne Shipping Co. Ltd.
						1985 Renamed Colne Phantom in April
						1987 Transferred to Claridge Trawlers Ltd.
						1992 Sold for scrapping.
						1992 Left Lowestoft on 6th January for Thames shipbreakers
						1992 Reported as sold to Caroline (Pty) Ltd., South Africa
						1992 Arrived at Lowestoft on 4th April, towed by Anglian Warrior
						1992 Left Lowestoft on 2nd May as Colne Phantom of Kingstown
						1992 Reported as returning to fishing off South Africa
Crystal Palace	Trawler	441	139 x 28 x 12	Diesel	1962	Built as GY683 for Rhondda Fishing Co. Ltd.
LT393	GHXM	147	Steel	8cyl 1120hp	Goole	1977 On charter to WFA
Lowestoft	303285			Mirrlees	Goole	1978 Bought by Colne Fishing Co. Ltd
					Shipbuilding	1978 Arrived at Lowestoft on 16th December
					& Repair	1979 Registered as LT393
						1981 Converted for use as a SSV
						1992 Sold for scrapping
						1992 Left Lowestoft on 2nd January for the shipbreakers
Culebra	Trawler	217	108 x 23 x 12	Diesel	1959	Launched as Midlothian
	MBUY	90	Steel	6cyl 540hp	Peterhead	1959 Completed as GN18 Lothian Leader
Lowestoft	300602			Ruston	Livingstone	1959 Owned by Lothian Trawling Co. Ltd. (BUT)
						1971 Company taken over by T. Davidson, Aberdeen
						1972 Became A163 Burnbanks
						1984 Sold to Colne Shipping Co. Ltd. for use as a SSV.
						1984 Arrived at Lowestoft on 4th. March.
						1984 Renamed Culebra in April
						1985 Sold for scrapping
						1985 Left Lowestoft on 24th April for the shipbreakers under tow
Cuttlefish	Trawler	152	94 x 22 x 8	Diesel	1959	Built for Claridge Trawler Ltd.
LT65	GDLE	54	Steel	6cyl 360hp	Thorne	1976 Converted for use as a SSV
Lowestoft	301513			Ruston	Richard Dunston	1981 Total loss on 30th. Nov. after grounding on Haisborough Sands

Name Fishing Registration Port of Registry	Vessel Type Call Sign RSS/Official No.	Gross Tonnage Net Tonnage	Dimensions (ft.) Construction	Propulsion Power Unit/ Make	Build Date Build Location Build Yard	History
Desirade Lowestoft	Trawler GHSS 303284	288 92	109 x 25 x 12 Steel	Diesel 5cyl 857hp Ruston	1961 Selby Cochrane	Built as GY678 Ross Kittiwake for Hudson Bros Trawlers Ltd . 1963 Transferred to G. F. Sleight & Sons Ltd 1968 Transferred to Ross Trawlers Ltd. 1970 Transferred to Goweroak Ltd. 1979 Converted for use as a SSV 1982 In the ownership of George Craig and Sons, Aberdeen 1982 Bought by Colne Shipping Co. Ltd., after chartering 1982 Arrived at Lowestoft during June 1991 Sold for scrapping to Spearings 1991 Left Lowestoft on 5th September for the shipbreakers
Dominica LT314 Lowestoft	Trawler MBHG 187038	212 72	106 x 23 x 13 Steel	Diesel 6cyl 403hp Ruston	1958 Grimsby J. S. Doig	Built for Drifter Trawlers Ltd. 1961 Top Trawler under Skipper Gallagher with earnings of £43,719 1982 Engine removed in November 1982 Renamed Ross Cormorant 1982/3 Sold for scrapping 1983 Left Lowestoft on 21st January for the shipbreakers at Gravesend
Dominica Lowestoft	Trawler MECN 303275	288 92	110 x 25 x 12 Steel	Diesel 857hp Ruston	1960 Selby Cochrane	Built as GY665 Ross Cormorant for Ross Trawlers Ltd. 1963 Transferred to G. F. Sleight & Sons Ltd. 1968 Transferred to Ross Trawlers Ltd. 1970 Transferred to Goweroak Ltd. 1979 Converted for use as a SSV 1982 In the ownership of George Craig and Sons, Aberdeen 1982 Arrived at Lowestoft on 17th. June 1982 Sold to Colne Shipping Co. Ltd., after chartering. 1982 Renamed Dominica. 1991 Sold for scrap to Chequers Iron and Steel Ltd. 1991 Left on 12th March for the shipbreakers towing Pagona
Enderby LT247	MFV MAEJ 166661	121 41	89 x 22 x 10 Wood	Diesel 4cyl 240hp Crossley	1946 Wivenhoe Wivenhoe Shipyard	Built as MFV1565 for the Admiralty 1947 Bought by E R. Harrison. Became GY491 Enderby 1951 Sold to Huxley Fishing Co. Ltd. 1951 Registered as LT247 1952 Sold to Norway. Became Maregg 1968 Renamed Arve Houden

Name Fishing Registration Port of Registry	Vessel Type Call Sign RSS/Official No.	Gross Tonnage Net Tonnage	Dimensions (ft.) Construction	Propulsion Power Unit/ Make	Build Date Build Location Build Yard	History
Eta LT400	MFV GFXY 166717	116 49	88 x 22 x 10 Wood	Diesel 4cyl 240hp Crossley	1944 Lowestoft Richards	Built as MFV1506 for the Admiralty 1948 Sold to G. D. Claridge 1948 Arrived at Lowestoft for conversion on 13th. May 1949 Transferred to Colne Fishing Co. Ltd. 1952 Transferred to Huxley Fishing Co. Ltd. 1952 Length reassessed to 92.5ft. 1954 Used for Drifting 1956 Sold to Putford Enterprises Ltd. 1957 Became LT400 Arduous 1958 Re-engined with 6cyl 360hp Ruston 1968 In use as a SSV 1969 Sold for use as a houseboat, later hulked
Eta Lowestoft	Tug 184927	52	65 x 17 x 6 Steel	Diesel 6cyl 360hp Ruston	1955 Knottingley John Harker	Built as Brenda Fisher for the Grimsby Salvage and Towing Co. Ltd. 1979 Bought by Colne Fishing Co. Ltd. from Grimsby Exchange. 1979 Arrived at Lowestoft on 18th. August 1979 Renamed Eta in September 1985 Engine removed 1985 Beached during March on north foreshore of Lake Lothing. 1986 Scrapping started in September and completed in November
Eta Lowestoft	Tug GQLE 305779	98	84 x 24 x 11 Steel	Diesel 2 x 6cyl 900hp Blackstone	1965 Hull St. Andrews Engineering	Built as Motorman for Humber Tugs Ltd. 1984 Sold to Klyne Winney Tugs Ltd., and became Anglianman 1988 Sold to Beesley Marine and became Clevelandman (unofficial) 1989 Sold to Colne Shipping Co. Ltd. and renamed Anglianman 1989 Started work for Colne Shipping on 2nd January 1989 Renamed Eta on 25th February, registered at Lowestoft 2000 A unit of the present Colne fleet
Exuma Lowestoft	Trawler GHTS 302407	165 61	93 x 22 x 10 Steel	Diesel 5cyl 475hp National	1961 Lowestoft Richards	Built as LT157 Boston Buccaneer for BDSF 1965 Transferred to Brixham Trawlers Ltd. 1973 Sold to C.V.Eastick Ltd., became LT157 Brave Buccaneer. 1975 Sold to Huxley Fishing Co. Ltd., renamed Exuma 1975 Converted for use as a SSV in October 1991 Sold for scrapping 1992 Left Lowestoft on 16th January for the shipbreakers
Equity I PD388	Drifter/Trawler MAVW 181489	119 51	86 x 20 x 11 Wood	Diesel 4cyl 265hp Crossley	1948 Oulton Broad Brooke Marine	Refer to Madame Prunier for history

Name Fishing Registration Port of Registry	Vessel Type Call Sign RSS/Official No.	Gross Tonnage Net Tonnage	Dimensions (ft.) Construction	Propulsion Power Unit/ Make	Build Date Build Location Build Yard	History
Fertile LT333	Drifter/Trawler 119619	98 38	87 x 18 x 9 Steel	Steam 32hp (200ihp) Compound Caledon	1907 Dundee Caledon S. & E	Built as PD169 Fertile for J. Buchan and others 1915 Sold to Irish owners, registration to LY37 1920 Sold to J. Buchan and others, registration to PD217 1942 Sold to new owner in Ayr, registration to AR1 1946 Sold to G. D. Claridge, registration to LT333 1949 Transferred to Colne Fishing Co. Ltd. 1952 Transferred to Clan Steam Fishing (Grimsby) Ltd. 1954 Sold for scrapping.
Fiskerton LT113	Trawler GIAP 303289	199 67	106 x 23 x 9 Steel	Diesel 6cyl 575hp Ruston	1962 Grimsby J. S. Doig	Built as GY676 Balmoral for Queen Steam Fishing Co. Ltd. 1964 Sold to Peter Sleight Trawlers Ltd., renamed Fiskerton 1975 Sold to Colne Fishing Co. Ltd., 1975 Arrived at Lowestoft on 23rd August 1975 Registered as LT113 1981 Sold for scrapping in July
Flora Taylor LT239	Drifter/Trawler GKGN 140844	95 40	86 x 18 x 9 Steel	Steam Triple 59hp Beardmore	1919 Oulton Broad J. W. Brooke	Built as HMD Moonset for the Admiralty 1920 Sold to Fishery Board for Scotland. 1920 Became PD444 Flora Taylor 1925 Sold to J. D. Irvin of North Shields 1930 Sold to R. V. Gouldby, registration changed to LT239 1939 Transferred to Mrs. L. E. Gouldby 1952 Sold to G. D. Claridge 1954 Sold for scrapping
Gillingham LT305 Lowestoft	Trawler GFHB 301821	427 139	139 x 28 x 12 Steel	Diesel 8cyl 1120hp Mirrlees	1960 Goole Goole Shipbuilding & Repair	Built as GY622 Gillingham for Wendover Fishing Co. (Grimsby) Ltd. 1978 Bought by Huxley Fishing Co. Ltd. 1978 Arrived at Lowestoft on 23rd June 1978 Registered as LT305 1981 Converted for use as a SSV 1987 Sold for scrap to Liguria Maritime 1987 Left Lowestoft on 8th July for the shipbreakers 1987 In the ownership of Liguria Maritime in November
Gordon David PW14	Beam Trawler NMHD6 B11862	 39	75 x 22 x 6 Steel	Diesel 230hp 172kw Caterpillar 3408	1991 Holland	Refer to PW14 Hannah Christine for history

Name Fishing Registration Port of Registry	Vessel Type Call Sign RSS/Official No.	Gross Tonnage Net Tonnage	Dimensions (ft.) Construction	Propulsion Power Unit/ Make	Build Date Build Location Build Yard	History
Grasby LT267	MFV MRXB 166664	112 44	88 x 22 x 10 Wood	Diesel 4cyl 240hp Crossley	1947 Charlestown Frank Curtis	Built as MFV1534 for the Admiralty 1947 Completed as GY510 Grasby for Shire Trawlers Ltd. 1951 Sold to Huxley Fishing Co. Ltd. 1951 Registered as LT267 1955 Sold to A. King & others. 1955 Became A66 Doonie Braes 1967 Owned by Metal Industries Ltd., Leith 1967 Converted for use as a salvage vessel 1967 During July working on the wreck of the S. S. Lusitania
Grayfish LT361 Lowestoft	Trawler MEGL 302397	160 55	94 x 22 x 8 Steel	Diesel 6cyl 410hp Ruston	1961 Thorne Richard Dunston	Built for the Huxley Fishing Co. Ltd. 1973 In use as a SSV 1973 Vessel grounded near Maesa, Shetlands on 21st. December 1974 Vessel declared a total loss
Grenada LT130 Lowestoft	Trawler MVWL 187000	205 70	105 x 23 x 9 Steel	Diesel 6cyl 403hp Ruston	1955 Selby Cochrane	Built for Dagon Fishing Co. Ltd. 1973 In use on SSV duties 1976 Fully converted for use as a SSV 1986 Sold for scrapping to G T Services at Barking 1986 Left Lowestoft in mid August for the shipbreakers
Guana Lowestoft	Trawler GFRU 301043	228 79	108 x 23 x 12 Steel	Diesel 6cyl 484hp Mirrlees	1960 Beverley Cook, Welton & Gemmell	Built as LO70 London Town for Hewett Fishing Co. Ltd., London 1981 Bought by Putford Enterprises Ltd. and BDSF 1981 Sold to Milford Haven 1984 Bought by Huxley Fishing Co. Ltd., for use as a SSV. 1984 Became Guana 1987 Sold to Pesca Fisheries Ltd. 1987 Left Lowestoft as LT378 on 30th July, towed by Montserrat
Guava GY272	Trawler GLRJ 162901	134 50	101 x 21 x 8 Steel	Diesel 6cyl 310hp Ruston	1935 Lowestoft Richards	Built as GY153 British Columbia for Grimsby Motor Trawlers Ltd. 1935 First successful large British diesel trawler 1939 Sold to the Admiralty and became T.118 - HMS Guava 1946 Sold to G. D. Claridge and registered as GY272 1949 Transferred to Colne Fishing Co. Ltd 1949 Became LT404 British Columbia 1952 Transferred to Clan Steam Fishing (Grimsby) Ltd. 1957 Vessel run down and sunk in North Sea. Crew safe.

Name Fishing Registration Port of Registry	Vessel Type Call Sign RSS/Official No.	Gross Tonnage Net Tonnage	Dimensions (ft.) Construction	Propulsion Power Unit/ Make	Build Date Build Location Build Yard	History
Guava LT73	Trawler GDNL 166722	309 106	128 x 26 x 12 Composite	Diesel 6cyl 540hp National	1945 Pembroke Dock Hancock	Built for the Admiralty as a MMS 1949 Sold to G.D.Claridge 1949 Became LT73 Guava 1949 Transferred to Claridge Trawlers Ltd. 1951 Tonnage reassessed to 285 gross 1953 Presumed lost with all hands on 31st. January
Gula LT179 Lowestoft	Drifter/Trawler GDXG 162991	81 33	75 x 20 x 7 Steel	Diesel 5cyl 150hp Ruston	1936 Lowestoft Richards	Built for LT(1934) Ltd. 1946 Sold to G.D.Claridge, Lowestoft 1949 Transferred to Colne Fishing Co. Ltd. 1955 Transferred to Dagon Fishing Co. Ltd. 1955 Chartered by MAFF with Rotha, for pair trawling experiment Extensively modernised during early 1960's 1973 Converted for use as a SSV 1986 Sold for scrapping 1986 Left Lowestoft for the shipbreakers on 4th July
Hannah Christine PW14	Beam Trawler NMHD6 B11832	39	75 x 22 x 6 Steel	Diesel 230hp 172kw Caterpiller 3408	1991 Holland	Built for David Evans of Padstow 1991 Entered service on 5th. April 1995 Sold to Colne Shipping Co. Ltd. in September 1996 Vessel renamed Gordon David during April 1998 Vessel sold to Leach Fishing Co. Ltd., Shoreham 1998 Left Lowestoft on 17th. December
Hosanna LT167	Drifter/Trawler GYRZ 149242	140 49	96 x 21 x 9 Steel	Diesel 6cyl 335hp Ruston	1930 Oulton Broad John Chambers	Built as a steam drifter/trawler for A. E. Beamish 1938 Winner of the Prunier Trophy with 238 crans 1939 Requisitioned by the Admiralty in November 1940 Assigned Pennant number FY950 and in use as a minesweeper 1944 Returned in November 1952 Sold to Milford Haven Coal Supplies Ltd. 1960 Sold to J. G. Mitchell 1960 Transferred to Scattan Ltd. 1960 Converted to diesel power by Richards Ironworks 1975 Sold to Colne Fishing Co. Ltd. during November 1976 Sold for scrapping at Oulton Broad

Name	Vessel Type	Gross Tonnage	Dimensions (ft.)	Propulsion	Build Date	History
Fishing Registration	Call Sign	Net Tonnage	Construction	Power Unit/	Build Location	
Port of Registry	RSS/Official No.			Make	Build Yard	

Huddersfield Town
LT259
Lowestoft

Trawler	439	139 x 28 x 12	Diesel	1962	1962 Built as GY702 for Wendover Fishing Co. (Grimsby) Ltd.
MFOP	146	Steel	8cyl 1120hp	Goole	1978 Bought by Huxley Fishing Co. Ltd.
304777			Ruston	Goole	1978 Arrived at Lowestoft on 13th July
				Shipbuilding	1978 Registered as LT259
				& Repair	1980 Converted for use as a SSV
					1991 Sold for scrapping
					1992 Left Lowestoft on 10th January for the shipbreakers

Inagua

Lowestoft

Trawler	288	109 x 25 x 10	Diesel	1961	Built as GY656 Ross Eagle for Ross Trawlers Ltd.
GHKW	92	Steel	5cyl 875hp	Selby	1962 Transferred to T. C. & F. Moss Ltd.
301850			Ruston	Cochrane	1966 Transferred to Ross Trawlers Ltd.
					1970 Transferred to Goweroak Ltd.
					1975 Converted for use as a SSV
					1982 In the ownership of George Craig and Sons, Aberdeen
					1982 Arrived at Lowestoft on 11th June
					1982 Sold to Colne Fishing Co. Ltd. after chartering
					1992 Sold for scrapping
					1992 Left Lowestoft on 13th January for the shipbreakers

Ira
LT269

Drifter/Trawler	114	85 x 22 x 9	Diesel	1951	Built as LT269 Bentley Queen for WHSN Co. Ltd.
GNFV	52	Steel	6cyl 230hp	Hessle	1960 Sold to Drifter Trawlers Ltd.
183979			Mirrlees	Henry Scarr	1960 Renamed Ira
					1969 Vessel offered for sale at £8500 during April
					1970 Sold to Pounds (Shipbreakers & Shipbrokers) Ltd.
					1970 Left Lowestoft on 17th December
					1971 Sold to Crossbow Shipping Co. Ltd., Leicester
					1975 Sold to Metal Recoveries Ltd., Newhaven
					1976 During April towed to a shipbreakers at Erith

Jamaica
LT185
Lowestoft

Trawler	285	128 x 25 x 12	Diesel	1947	Built as A425 Star of Scotland for Walker Steam Fishing Co. Ltd.
MRRV	98	Steel	5cyl 700hp	Aberdeen	1959 Sold to Dagon Fishing Co. Ltd.
182015			British Polar	Hall Russell	1959 Arrived at Lowestoft during December.
					1960 Became LT185 Jamaica
					1972 During October fully converted for use as a SSV
					1976 Sold for scrapping.
					1976 Left Lowestoft on 5th July bound for Belcon Trading Co. Ltd. at Queenborough

Name Fishing Registration Port of Registry	Vessel Type Call Sign RSS/Official No.	Gross Tonnage Net Tonnage	Dimensions (ft.) Construction	Propulsion Power Unit/ Make	Build Date Build Location Build Yard	History
Jamaica Lowestoft	Trawler GXPL 187864	426 139	139 x 28 x 14 Steel	Diesel 8cyl 1000hp Mirrlees	1958 Goole Goole Shipbuilding & Repair	Built as FD208 Broadwater for Mason Trawlers Ltd. 1960 Transferred to Broadwater Trawlers Ltd. 1964 Transferred to BDSF 1965 Transferred to Iago Steam Trawling Co. Ltd 1972 Renamed Boston Crusader 1976 Bought by Drifter Trawlers Ltd. 1976/7 Became Jamaica. Converted for use as a SSV 1986 Sold for scrapping in December.
Kennedy Lowestoft	Trawler GXBP 187861	426 139	139 x 28 x 14 Steel	Diesel 8cyl 1000hp Mirrlees	1957 Goole Goole Shipbuilding & Repair	Built as FD139 Boston Britannia for BDSF 1964 Transferred to North Cape Fishing Co. Ltd. 1969 Sold to Heward Trawlers Ltd. Became Kennedy 1976 Bought by Colne Fishing Co. Ltd. 1976 Arrived at Lowestoft on 17th June 1976 Allocated fishing registration LT439 1976 Converted for use as a SSV during August 1976 Started work as a SSV on 14th August 1986 Sold for scrapping to G T Services at Barking 1986 Left Lowestoft on 20th June for the breakers with Bahama
Kingfish LT186 Lowestoft	Trawler MVZD 187001	151 49	94 x 22 x 8 Steel	Diesel 6cyl 360hp Ruston	1955 Thorne Richard Dunston	Built for Claridge Trawlers Ltd. 1955 Arrived at Lowestoft on 24th August 1967 Re-engined with 6cyl 360hp engine from Yellowtail 1970 Converted for use as a SSV 1979 Re-engined again in November 1986 Sold for scrapping to G T Services at Barking 1986 Left Lowestoft on 14th August towing British Honduras
Kristin LT68	MFV MRRN 181319	113 58	87 x 22 x 8 Wood	Diesel 4cyl 240hp Crossley	1943 Totnes Frank Curtis	Refer to LT68 Albacore for history

Name Fishing Registration Port of Registry	Vessel Type Call Sign RSS/Official No.	Gross Tonnage Net Tonnage	Dimensions (ft.) Construction	Propulsion Power Unit/ Make	Build Date Build Location Build Yard	History
Lady Cora Lowestoft	Trawler MXBL 184945	238 81	111 x 25 x 12 Steel	Diesel 6cyl 528hp Widdop	1956 Aberdeen John Lewis	Built as GY333 Boston Valetta for Don Fishing Co. Ltd. 1961 Transferred to Acadia Fisheries Ltd., Halifax, Nova Scotia 1961 Became Acadia Fin-Fare 1962 Registered as St.John's 12 1968 Transferred to BDSF, became LT256 Boston Valetta. 1971 Sold to Pounds (Shipbreakers and Shipbrokers) Ltd., Portsmouth 1972 Transferred to Pounds Marine Shipping Ltd., Havant 1973 Owned by Blythe Securities Ltd., London. 1973 Sold to Dunedale Ltd., 28 Victoria Street, Douglas 1973 Became Lady Cora 1974 Arrived at Lowestoft on 18th January 1974 Painted in Colne colours during February 1974 Colne colours removed from vessel in July 1976 For sale in May by order of Admiralty Marshal 1976 Sold for scrapping to T. G. Darling, Oulton Broad.
Lady Luck R355	Drifter/Trawler MFPD 137724	92 39	87 x 18 x 9 Steel	Steam 34hp	1920 Montrose	Built for Robert Frater, 21 Trevor Square, Knightsbridge, SW 7 1929 In the ownership of Char Steam Trawling Co. Ltd. 1944 Took part in rescue of survivors from torpedoed HMS Warwick 1946 In the ownership of Drifter Trawlers Ltd., Milford Haven. 1957 Drifter Trawlers Ltd. became part of the Colne Group 1957 Sold for scrapping
Lass O' Doune SA116	Drifter/Trawler GWVC 127317	92 35	86 x 18 x 9 Steel	Steam 41hp Compound	1910 Aberdeen Hall Russell	Built as BF236 Lass O' Doune for George Falconer and others 1914 Sold to John J. George 1915-1919 Chartered by Admiralty at £55.12s.6d per mouth 1920 Sold to Steam Pilot Boat Co. Ltd., Pilotage Office, Cardiff 1942 Sold to Ministry of War Transport 1943 Sold to Swansea owners, registered as SA116 1945 Bought by G. D. Claridge 1946 Total loss on 14th October after sinking off Shoreham
Loch Laoi LT332	Trawler MDZU 302381	106 65	88 x 21 x 9 Steel	Diesel 5cyl 280hp Lister Blackstone	1949 Germany	Built as Hermann Leymann for Flehr & Co., Bremerhaven 1953 Bought by An Bord Iascaigh Mhain, Became D409 Loch Laoi 1960 Sold to Claridge Trawlers Ltd. Registered as LT332 1960 Arrived at Lowestoft on 4th July 1969 Vessel offered for sale at £8500 in April 1970 Sold for scrapping 1970 Left on 2nd June for the shipbreakers at Blyth with LT335

Name Fishing Registration Port of Registry	Vessel Type Call Sign RSS/Official No.	Gross Tonnage Net Tonnage	Dimensions (ft.) Construction	Propulsion Power Unit/ Make	Build Date Build Location Build Yard	History
Loch Lein LT334	Trawler MDZH 302382	103 67	88 x 21 x 9 Steel	Diesel 5cyl 250hp Lister Blackstone	1948 Germany	Built as Rheinland for Flehr & Co., Bremerhaven 1953 Bought by An Bord Iascaigh Mhain. Became D411 Loch Lein 1960 Sold to Claridge Trawlers Ltd. Registered as LT334 1960 Arrived at Lowestoft on 16th. July 1963 Sold to Captain Walter Holmes of Fleetwood. 1965 Caught fire on 17th. March at Ayr, later rebuilt 1967 Registered in Auckland, New Zealand in February 1968 Registered at Lowestoft, England in September 1968 Registered at Auckland, New Zealand in November 1970 Sold to Auckland Seine Boat Association Ltd. 1972 Sold to Anette Dwerryhouse & others, Auckland 1975 Sold to Jaybel Nicheme Ltd., Auckland 1976 Sold to Rope Shipping Co. Ltd., Auckland 1988 Sank off the Australian coast
Loch Lorgan LT335	Trawler MEAA 302383	106 65	88 x 21 x 9 Steel	Diesel 5cyl 280hp Lister Blackstone	1949 Germany	Built as Martin Schilling for Flehr & Co., Bremerhaven 1953 Bought by An Bord Iascaigh Mhain. Became D413 Loch Lorgan 1960 Sold to Claridge Trawlers Ltd., registered as LT335 1960 Arrived at Lowestoft on 23rd. July 1969 Vessel offered for sale at £8500 in April 1970 Sold for scrapping 1970 Left on 2nd June for the shipbreakers at Blyth with LT332
Madame Prunier LT343	Drifter/Trawler MAVW 181489 .	119 51	86 x 20 x 11 Wood	Diesel 4cyl 265hp Crossley	1948 Oulton Broad Brooke Marine	Launched as Madame Prunier Completed as PD388 Equity I for the Scottish CWS Ltd. 1952 Bought by Clan Steam Fishing Co.(Grimsby) Ltd 1952 Registered as LT343 1953 Renamed Madame Prunier. 1953 Sold to Pevensey Castle Ltd. 1959 Sold to G. Doyle, Howth 1961 Renamed Croidte Au Duin 1966 Registered as N198 1968 Registered as D190 1990 Vessel scrapped at Kilkeel

Name Fishing Registration Port of Registry	Vessel Type Call Sign RSS/Official No.	Gross Tonnage Net Tonnage	Dimensions (ft.) Construction	Propulsion Power Unit/ Make	Build Date Build Location Build Yard	History
Maravanne LT326	MFV MAYN 180190	119 43	92 x 23 x 10 Steel	Diesel 4cyl 240hp Crossley	1945 Looe Frank Curtis	Built as MFV1529 for the Admiralty 1948 Sold and became PH155 Maravanne 1948 Sold to Joseph Craig, Aberdeen, registered as A621 1952 Sold to Clan Steam Fishing Co.(Grimsby) Ltd. 1952 Registered as LT326 1958-59 Extensively modernised by Richards Ironworks Ltd. 1958-59 Re-engined with a 6cyl 360hp Ruston, became Yellowtail 1968 Advertised for sale complete with Ruston 6VEBM engine 1970 Sold to Mr. S. Gooch for use as a houseboat 1976 Vessel moored near Mutford Lock, Oulton Broad on 7th January 1979 Vessel sank at Mutford Lock during January 1987 Vessel raised and beached on shore of Lake Lothing 2000 Vessel still beached and decaying.
Mardyke Lowestoft	Tug 181393	37	57 x 17 x 5 Steel	Diesel 6cyl 302hp Ruston	1957 Appledore P. K. Harris	Built as John Henry of Grimsby 1960 Bought by the Port of London Authority, renamed Mardyke 1970 Sold to R.E.Trim Ltd. 1970 Sold to Colne Fishing Co. Ltd., registered at Lowestoft 1973 Became a total loss after being stranded on Corton Sand trying to refloat Grenada.
Martinique Lowestoft	Trawler GSSR 184925	254 88	118 x 25 x 12 Steel	Diesel 4cyl 640hp British Polar	1955 Selby Cochrane	Built as GY112 Thessalonian for Sir Thomas Robinson & Sons Ltd. 1976 Bought by Dagon Fishing Co. Ltd. 1976 Arrived at Lowestoft on 6th November 1976 Allocated fishing registration LT272 1977 Converted for use as a SSV, became Matinique. 1986 Sold for scrapping to Cook Bros., New Holland 1987 Left on 22nd January for the shipbreakers with Tobago

Name Fishing Registration Port of Registry	Vessel Type Call Sign RSS/Official No.	Gross Tonnage Net Tonnage	Dimensions (ft.) Construction	Propulsion Power Unit/ Make	Build Date Build Location Build Yard	History
Merbreeze LT365	Drifter/Trawler MAEP 162956	122 42	94 x 20 x 9 Steel	Diesel 6cyl 335hp Ruston	1931 Lowestoft Richards	Built as the steam drifter/trawler LT253 Merbreeze for A. H. Watson. 1931 The last coal burning drifter/trawler built for Lowestoft 1932 Transferred to P. W. Watson & Sons Ltd. 1939 Requisitioned by the Admiralty in November 1940 Assigned Pennant number FY953 and in use as a minesweeper 1946 Returned and registered as LT365 1955 Sold to Breeze Co. (Lowestoft) Ltd. 1957 Sold to C. H. J. Eastick 1959 Sold to Merbreeze Ltd 1959 Converted to diesel power by Richards Ironworks 1975 Sold to Colne Fishing Co. Ltd. during November 1976 Sold for scrapping at Oulton Broad
Mill O'Buckie R129	Drifter/Trawler GKSD 132166	94 41	86 x 19 x 9 Steel	Steam 42hp	1914 Aberdeen	1923 In the ownership of the Invicta T. & F. Co. Ltd., Ramsgate 1929 In the ownership of Char Steam Trawling Co. Ltd. 1941 Requisitioned by Admiralty 1942 In service on Harbour Service duties. 1945 Returned to owner 1946 In the ownership of Drifter Trawlers Ltd., Milford Haven 1957 Drifter Trawlers Ltd., became part of the Colne Group. 1957 At Lowestoft on 3rd March 1957 R355 Lucky Lady seen on lifebelts and small boat 1957 Left Lowestoft in mid March for shipbreakers in Bruges
Montserrat LT64 Lowestoft	Trawler GDGA 301512	228 82	105 x 24 x 10 Steel	Diesel 6cyl 403hp Ruston	1959 Selby Cochrane	Built for Huxley Fishing Co. Ltd. 1960 Top Trawler under Skipper Harper with earnings of £43,408 1976 Converted for use as a SSV 1987 Sold to Pesca Fisheries Ltd. 1987 Left Lowestoft on 30th July as LT376 towing the Guana

Name	Vessel Type	Gross Tonnage	Dimensions (ft.)	Propulsion	Build Date	History
Fishing Registration	Call Sign	Net Tonnage	Construction	Power Unit/	Build Location	
Port of Registry	RSS/Official No.			Make	Build Yard	

Mustique	Trawler	254	118 x 25 x 12	Diesel	1954	Built as GY92 Olivean for Sir Thomas Robinson & Sons (GY) Ltd.
	GSPD	82	Steel	4cyl 640hp	Selby	1976 Transferred to WFA
Lowestoft	184923			British Polar	Cochrane	1976 Sold to Dagon Fishing Co. Ltd., Luton
						1976 Arrived at Lowestoft on 27th November
						1977 Allocated fishing registration LT392
						1977 Converted for use as a SSV, renamed Mustique in March
						1978 Arrived at Falmouth on 16th December with engine trouble
						1978 Towed home from Falmouth
						1979 Laid up with serious engine problems at Brooke Marine
						1981 Exchanged identity with GY693 Ross Heron
						1981 Sold for scrapping in October as Ross Heron
						1982 Left Lowestoft on 21st January bound for the shipbreakers.
Mustique	Trawler	288	110 x 25 x 12	Diesel	1962	Built as GY693 Ross Heron for Ross Trawlers Ltd.
	GHZC	92	Steel	6cyl 875hp	Selby	1970 Transferred to Goweroak Ltd.
Lowestoft	303290			Ruston	Cochrane	1979 Converted for use as a SSV
						1981 Sold to Dagon Fishing Co. Ltd.
						1981 Arrived at Lowestoft on 29th. August
						1981 Exchanged identity with the SSV Mustique
						1991 Sold for scrap as Mustique
						1991 Left Lowestoft on 29th. Sept. for the shipbreakers towing Colne Hunter.
Nevis	Trawler	468	163 x 28 x 14	Diesel	1958	Built as the steam trawler GY60 Kelvin for Derwent Trawlers Ltd.
	GBHX	159	Steel	6cyl 1440hp	Selby	1960 Transferred to Ross Trawlers Ltd.
Lowestoft	168603			Ruston	Cochrane	1961 Transferred to Yorkshire Trawlers Ltd.
						1962 Transferred to G. F. Sleight & Sons Ltd.
						1962 Renamed Ross Kelvin
						1966/7 Lengthened from 139ft. to 163ft., converted to diesel power
						1969 Transferred to Ross Trawlers Ltd.
						1970 Transferred to Goweroak Ltd.
						1981 Converted for use as a SSV
						1981 On charter to Colne Shipping Co. Ltd., became Nevis
						1982 In the ownership of George Craig and Sons, Aberdeen
						1982 Sold to Colne Shipping Co. Ltd.
						1982 Allocated registration LT60
						1987 Sold for scrapping. Given registration LT168
						1987 Left Lowestoft on 28th September bound for the shipbreakers

Name Fishing Registration Port of Registry	Vessel Type Call Sign RSS/Official No.	Gross Tonnage Net Tonnage	Dimensions (ft.) Construction	Propulsion Power Unit/ Make	Build Date Build Location Build Yard	History
Notts Forest LT346 Lowestoft	Trawler GHDJ 301839	441 147	139 x 28 x 12 Steel	Diesel 8cyl 1120hp Mirrless	1960 Goole Goole Shipbuilding & Repair	Built as GY649 Notts Forest for Rhondda Fishing Co. Ltd. 1978 Bought by Colne Fishing Co. Ltd. 1978 Arrived at Lowestoft on 6th July 1978 Registered as LT346 1981 Converted for use as a SSV 1991 Sold for scrap. 1991 Left Lowestoft on 16th December bound for the shipbreakers
Pagona Lowestoft	Trawler GHKX 301854	288 92	110 x 25 x 12 Steel	Diesel 4cyl 875hp Ruston	1961 Selby Cochrane	Built as GY657 Ross Hawk for Ross Trawlers Ltd. 1962 Transferred to G. F. Sleight & Sons Ltd. 1968 Transferred to Ross Trawlers Ltd. 1970 Transferred to Goweroak Ltd. 1976 Converted for use as a SSV 1982 In the ownership of George Craig and Sons, Aberdeen 1982 Arrived at Lowestoft on 6th June 1982 Bought by Colne Fishing Co. Ltd. after chartering 1991 Sold for scrapping to Chequers Ion and Steel Ltd. 1991 Left for the shipbreakers on 12th March towed by Dominica
Patria LT178	Drifter/Trawler GYVX	140 66	102 x 20 x 9 Steel	Steam 250hp Triple Burgerhaut	1916 Holland	Built for Dutch owners as the Atlantic 1930 Sold to J. C. Hayward, 9 Denes Rd., & others, 1930 Registered as LT178 1939 Transferred to Kittiwake Ltd. 1946 Transferred to Jack Breach Ltd. 1947 Winner of Prunier Trophy with 253 crans 1954 Sold to Colne Fishing Co. Ltd. 1954 Sold for scrapping. 1954 Left Lowestoft on 3rd August bound for the shipbreakers
Port Vale LT309 Lowestoft	Trawler MXWY 181392	427 140	139 x 28 x 12 Steel	Diesel 8cyl 1120hp Ruston	1957 Goole Goole Shipbuilding & Repair	Built as GY484 for Wendover Fishing Co. (Grimsby) Ltd. 1975 Transferred to Consolidated Fisheries Ltd. 1978 Bought by Colne Fishing Co. Ltd. 1978 Arrived at Lowestoft on 29th July 1978 Fishing off West Coast, landing at Hull 1981 Converted for use as a SSV 1986 Sold for scrapping to Liguria Maritime 1987 Left Lowestoft on 7th January bound for the shipbreakers

Name Fishing Registration Port of Registry	Vessel Type Call Sign RSS/Official No.	Gross Tonnage Net Tonnage	Dimensions (ft.) Construction	Propulsion Power Unit/ Make	Build Date Build Location Build Yard	History
Real Madrid GY674	Trawler MEIP 303279	441 147	139 x 28 x 12 Steel	Diesel 8cyl 1120hp Ruston	1961 Goole Goole Shipbuilding & Repair	Built as GY674 for Rhondda Fishing Co. Ltd. 1978 Bought by Colne Fishing Co. Ltd. 1979/80 Stripped for spares 1981 Sold for scrapping
Red Snapper LT303	MFV MLVL 181588	116 41	88 x 22 x 10 Steel	Diesel 4cyl 240hp Ruston	1945 Par Frank Curtis	Refer to LT303 Snapper for history
Rewga LT234 Lowestoft	Drifter/Trawler GDRG 163002	81 36	75 x 20 x 7 Steel	Diesel 5cyl 150hp Ruston	1937 Lowestoft Richards	1947 Bought by G.D.Claridge 1949 Transferred to Colne Fishing Co. Ltd 1955 Lengthened to 82 x 20 x 7. Gross tonnage to 81 1955 Re-engined with 5cyl 220hp Ruston. Extensively modernised in the early 1960's In later years used as a SSV 1971 Sold to T.G.Darling at Oulton Broad for scrapping. 1971 Delivered to shipbreakers yard on 6th October
Rewga Lowestoft	Drifter/Trawler MWVG 186405	112 63	91 x 21 x 10 Steel	Diesel 6cyl 360hp Ruston	1956 Lowestoft Richards	Built as YH77 Ocean Dawn for Bloomfields Ltd., Gt.Yarmouth 1963 Bought by E.A.I. & C.S. Ltd. 1963 Registered LT466 on the 21st February 1968 Transferred to Small & Co. (Lowestoft) Ltd. in February 1969 Sold to John Muir, Anstruther. 1969 Sailed for Scotland on the 2nd. September 1969 Registered as KY371 1979 On 10th September sank in Aberdeen. 1979 Raised on the 19th September 1984 Sold to Colne Shipping Co. Ltd. in March 1984 Converted for use as a SSV, renamed Rewga 1987 Sold to Mats Lilja, Sweden 1987 Left Lowestoft on 24th February bound for Sweden 1988 Renamed Ocean Dawn 1991 Advertised for sale at £65,000 in the spring 1991 Advertised for sale at £45,000 in September 1998 Sold to Mr. J. Price, Shoreham

| Name | Vessel Type | Gross Tonnage | Dimensions (ft.) | Propulsion | Build Date | History |
| Fishing Registration | Call Sign | Net Tonnage | Construction | Power Unit/ | Build Location | |
Port of Registry	RSS/Official No.			Make	Build Yard	
Rockfish	Trawler	151	94 x 22 x 8	Diesel	1956	Built for Huxley Fishing Co. Ltd.
LT244	MWZD	50	Steel	6cyl 360hp	Thorne	1969 Converted for use as a SSV in November
Lowestoft	187012			Ruston	Richard Dunston	1986 Sold for scrapping to G T Services at Barking
						1986 Left Lowestoft on 16th July bound for the shipbreakers
Ross Cormorant	Trawler	212	106 x 23 x 13	Diesel	1958	See LT314 Dominica for history
	MBHG	72	Steel	6cyl 403hp	Grimsby	
Lowestoft	187038			Ruston	J.S.Doig	
Ross Heron	Trawler	254	118 x 25 x 12	Diesel	1954	See Mustique (formerly Olivean) for history
	GSPD	82	Steel	4cyl 640hp	Selby	
Lowestoft	184923			British Polar	Cochrane	
Rotha	Drifter/Trawler	78	75 x 21 x 8	Diesel	1937	Built for LT (1934) Ltd.
LT208	GDXD	34	Steel	5cyl 150hp	Lowestoft	1944 Became Elfin for base ship duties
Lowestoft	162996			Ruston	Richards	1947 Sold to G. D. Claridge
						1949 Transferred to Colne Fishing Co. Ltd.
						1955 Lengthened to 82ft. from 75ft. Gross tonnage to 81
						1955 Chartered with Gula by MAFF for pair trawling experiment
						1955 Re-engined with 5cyl 220hp Ruston
						Extensively modernised in the early 1960's
						1971 Converted for use as a SSV
						1986 Sold for scrapping to G T Services, Barking.
						1986 Left Lowestoft on 9th July bound for the shipbreakers
Saltrou	Trawler	281	121 x 26 x 13	Diesel	1960	Built as A417 Clova for Clova Fishing Co. Ltd. (BUT)
	GHBU	94	Steel	4cyl 640hp	Aberdeen	1975/6 Converted for use as a SSV
Lowestoft	301593			British Polar	John Lewis	1982 In the ownership of George Craig and Sons, Aberdeen
						1982 Sold to Colne Shipping Co. Ltd. Became Saltrou
						1986 Sold to Warbler Shipping Ltd. in December.
						1987 Became Dawn Saviour
						1987 Re-engined with 8cyl 660hp Blackstone
						1993 Sold to Middle East Interests
						1993 Left Lowestoft on 4th July as Seaguard, bound for Israel.

Name	Vessel Type	Gross Tonnage	Dimensions (ft.)	Propulsion	Build Date	History
Fishing Registration	Call Sign	Net Tonnage	Construction	Power Unit/	Build Location	
Port of Registry	RSS/Official No.			Make	Build Yard	

Samarian	Trawler	331	131 x 27 x 12	Diesel	1957	Built as GY445 Samarian for the Onward Steam Fishing Co. Ltd.
	GVYZ	110	Steel	5cyl 950hp	Selby	1976 Bought by Colne Fishing Co. Ltd.
Lowestoft	181382			British Polar	Cochrane	1976 Arrived at Lowestoft on 21st. October.
						1977 Registered as LT545 in March
						1977 Converted for use as a SSV.
						1977 Developed serious engine problems off the Shetlands
						1977 Towed home in November from the Shetlands and laid up.
						1979 Left Lowestoft on 13th August for the breakers under tow
Sawfish	Trawler	152	94 x 22 x 8	Diesel	1959	Built for Dagon Fishing Co. Ltd.
LT66	MCAQ	54	Steel	6cyl 360hp	Thorne	1976 In use as a SSV
Lowestoft	301517			Ruston	Richard Dunston	1987 Sold to Pesca Fisheries for use as a fishing vessel.
						1987 Left Lowestoft on 12th. October as LT375
Scampton	Trawler	214	109 x 24 x 9	Diesel	1962	Built as GY166 for Peter Sleight Trawlers Ltd.
LT110	GHLW	72	Steel	6cyl 655hp	Hessle	1968 Re-engined. 622hp Ruston replaced by a 655hp unit
Lowestoft	301849			Ruston	Richard Dunston	1975 Sold to Colne Fishing Co. Ltd.
						1975 Arrived at Lowestoft on 21st. August
						1975 Registered as LT110
						1981 Converted for use as a SSV
						1991 Sold for scrapping to Spearings
						1991 Left Lowestoft on 19th September for the shipbreakers
Silverfish	Trawler	160	94 x 22 x 8	Diesel	1961	Built for Huxley Fishing Co. Ltd.
LT340	GHST	55	Steel	6cyl 410hp	Thorne	1977 Converted for use as a SSV
Lowestoft	302401			Ruston	Richard Dunston	1987 Sold to Spain
						1987 Left Lowestoft as LT136 on 12th March
						1990 Sold and registered in Panama as Antoko
						1991 Wrecked during August

| Name | Vessel Type | Gross Tonnage | Dimensions (ft.) | Propulsion | Build Date | History |
| Fishing Registration | Call Sign | Net Tonnage | Construction | Power Unit/ | Build Location | |
Port of Registry	RSS/Official No.			Make	Build Yard	
Snapper	MFV	116	88 x 22 x 10	Diesel	1945	Built as MFV1532 for the Admiralty
LT303	MLVL	41	Wood	4cyl 240hp	Par	1947 Sold and became Herm Coast of Guernsey
	181588			Crossley	Frank Curtis	1947 Registered in London
						1948 Sold to Tilbrook Trawlers Ltd. Became M304 Sea Monarch
						1952 Sold to Huxley Fishing Co. Ltd. Became LT303 Red Snapper
						1953 Renamed Snapper
						1960 Extensively modernised by Richards Ironworks Ltd.
						1960 Re-engined with a 6cyl 360hp Ruston
						1962 Sold to Amalgamated Fisheries (Pty) Ltd., Capetown
						1962 Registered CTA300
						1968 Caught fire in Durban Harbour
						1968 Leaking badly on 16th October off St. Lucia Light. Abandoned
						1968 Found in waterlogged condition during December
						1968 Grounded in Richards Bay, vessel broken up on site
Spearfish	Trawler	151	94 x 22 x 8	Diesel	1956	Built for Claridge Trawlers Ltd.
LT232	GVGT	50	Steel	6cyl 360hp	Thorne	1971 In use on SSV duties
Lowestoft	187009			Ruston	Richard Dunston	1976 Fully converted for use as a SSV
						1983 Partially sank after a collision in the English Channel
						1983 Sunk by gunfire on 29th. June after becoming a hazard
Spurs	Trawler	439	139 x 28 x 12	Diesel	1962	Built as GY697 for Wendover Fishing Co. (Grimsby) Ltd.
	GJZU	146	Steel	8cyl 1200hp	Goole	1978 Bought by Huxley Fishing Co. Ltd
Lowestoft.	303300			Mirrlees	Goole	1978 Arrived at Lowestoft on 22nd July
					Shipbuilding	1980 Converted for use as SSV, after 20 months of being laid up
					& Repair	1991 Left Lowestoft on 12th July bound for the shipbreakers
SSAFA	Trawler	428	139 x 28 x 14	Diesel	1958	Built as FD155 SSAFA for BDSF
LT73	MXYY	139	Steel	8cyl 1000hp	Goole	1961 Ran aground on Island of Coll and abandoned for many weeks
Lowestoft	187863			Mirrlees	Goole	1965 Transferred to Parbel-Smith Ltd.
					Shipbuilding	1969 Sold to West Coast Salvage & Contracting Co. Ltd., Vancouver
					& Repair	1970 Sold to BDSF
						1971 Sold to Heward Trawlers Ltd.
						1975 Bought by Huxley Fishing Co. Ltd.
						1975 Arrived at Lowestoft on 31st July
						1975 Registration changed from FD155 to LT73 in October
						1977 Converted for use as a SSV
						1987 Sold for scrapping to Liguria Maritime
						1987 Left Lowestoft on 12th July for the shipbreakers as LT154
						1987 In the ownership of Liguria Maritime in November

Name Fishing Registration Port of Registry	Vessel Type Call Sign RSS/Official No.	Gross Tonnage Net Tonnage	Dimensions (ft.) Construction	Propulsion Power Unit/ Make	Build Date Build Location Build Yard	History
St. Andrew LT335	Beam Trawler GGCH A18974	218 79	115 x 25 x 13 Steel	Diesel 1300hp 970kw Atlas	1975 Holland	Built as UK33 Eize Willem Fokke for Jac Hoekstyra 1986 Bought by Colne Shipping Co. Ltd. 1986 Arrived at Lowestoft on 26th March 1986 Became LT335 St. Andrew in April 1994/5 Decommissioned and scrapped at Lowestoft.
St. Anne Lowestoft	Trawler GJKU 303809	622 186	167 x 30 x 16 Steel	Diesel 8cyl 1400hp 1030kw Mirrlees	1962 Beverley Cook, Welton & Gemmell	Built as H261 Lord St. Vincent for Lord Line Ltd. 1966 Transferred to Hellyer Bros. Ltd. 1980 Bought by Colne Fishing Co. Ltd. 1980 Arrived at Lowestoft on 15th March 1980 Converted for use as a SSV, renamed St. Anne 1992 Sold during December and continued to be used as a SSV 1998 Renamed Veesea Hawk
St. Anthony LT1005	Beam Trawler MYOK4 C16613	498 149	138 x 28 x 17 Steel	Diesel 9cyl 2000hp 1471kw Deutz	1999 Poland/Holland	1999 Built for Colne Shipping Co. Ltd. 1999 Arrived at Lowestoft on 27th March 1999 First landing on 12th April. 1999 Landed 22574kg on 12th April and grossed £38,103 2000 A unit of the present Lowestoft fleet
St. Christopher LT340	Beam Trawler PGTC A18979	324 132	131 x 26 x 12 Steel	Diesel 8cyl 1760hp 1380kw Deutz	1975 Holland	1975 Launched as LE62 Pietertje Elisabeth 1975 Owned by Rederij J. Toering & Zn B.V. 1978 Lengthened from 120ft. to 131ft., tonnage 283 to 324. 1986 Bought by Colne Shipping Co. Ltd. 1986 Arrived at Lowestoft on 3rd June 1986 First fishing trip from Lowestoft on 3rd July 1987 Top Trawler under Skippers Athorn/Whitlam 1987 Vessel earned £845,435 1988 Top Trawler under Skipper Athorn with earnings of £740,295 1994 Decommissioned and scrapped at Lowestoft in November
St.Claude LT714	Trawler GHHC 301835	310 110	115 x 25 x 13 Steel	Diesel 6cyl 750hp Mirrlees	1960 Portsmouth Vospers	Built as GY628 Haselbech for Grimsby Near Water Trawlers Ltd. 1966 Arrived at Lowestoft on 17th. September 1967 Became LT714 Boston Shackleton in April 1982 Sold to Colne Shipping Co. Ltd. Became St.Claude 1986 Sold for scrapping to G T Services at Barking 1986 Left Lowestoft on 15th July bound for the shipbreakers

Name Fishing Registration Port of Registry	Vessel Type Call Sign RSS/Official No.	Gross Tonnage Net Tonnage	Dimensions (ft.) Construction	Propulsion Power Unit/ Make	Build Date Build Location Build Yard	History
St.Claude LT714	Beam Trawler MKJV9 B10470	266 79	117 x 25 x 13 Steel	Diesel 8cyl 1800hp 1324kw Deutz	1981 Holland	Built as GO8 Eben Haezer for Rodert and Son 1989 Bought by Colne Shipping Co. Ltd. 1989 Arrived at Lowestoft on 22nd. March 1989 Became LT714 St.Claude 2000 A unit of the present Lowestoft fleet
St.Croix LT251	Trawler GHHF 301846	310 110	115 x 25 x 11 Steel	Diesel 6cyl 750hp Mirrlees	1960 Portsmouth Vospers	Built as GY465 Parkroyd for Fleetwood Near Water Trawlers Ltd. 1969 Sold to North Star Steam Fishing Co. Ltd. 1969 Registered as A161 1976 Sold to Colne Fishing Co. Ltd. 1976 Arrived at Lowestoft on 11th. January 1976 First landing at Lowestoft on 4th February 1976 Became LT251 St.Croix 1986 Sold for scrapping to Henderson and Morez, Gravesend 1986 Left Lowestoft on 27th January under tow for the shipbreakers
St.Croix LT332	Beam Trawler GFTG A18973	240 72	116 x 25 x 11 Steel	Diesel 6cyl 1320hp 984kw Deutz	1974 Belgium	1974 Launched as KW105 Maarten for H.Van Duyn of Katwijk 1976 Sold to Rederij Atlas and became Z105 Atlas 1985 Sold to Colne Shipping Co. Ltd. 1985 Arrived at Lowestoft on 14th. December 1986 Registered as LT332, first fishing trip in February 1986 Fished as LT332 Atlas until 10th April 1986 Renamed St.Croix after 10th April 1994/5 Decommissioned and scrapped at Lowestoft
St.Davids LT494	Trawler GSLH 181298	320 110	137 x 26 x 14 Steel	Diesel 6cyl 1100hp Ruston	1947 Beverley Cook, Welton & Gemmell	Built as H420 Allan Water for the Great Western Fishing Co. Ltd. 1948 Bought by J.V.Pronk NV of Ijmuiden. Registered as IJM34. 1964 Sold to Claridge Trawlers Ltd. Registered as LT494 1964 Arrived at Lowestoft on 21st August 1965 Renamed St.Davids 1966 Re-engined, a 6cyl 1100hp Ruston replacing her 930hp Ruston 1980 Sold for scrapping in July 1980 Left Lowestoft for the shipbreakers in September
St.Davids Lowestoft	Trawler GJTJ 304780	576 194	166 x 30 x 16 Steel	Diesel 8cyl 1400hp 1030kw Mirrlees	1962 Beverley Cook, Welton & Gemmell	Built as GY704 Northern Gift for Northern Trawlers Ltd. 1971 Transferred to Ross Trawlers Ltd. 1980 Bought by Dagon Fishing Co. Ltd 1980 Arrived at Lowestoft in December 1981/82 Converted for use as a SSV 1987 Sold for scrapping. Given fishing registration LT90 1987 Towed by Caicos on 28th September to the breakers

Name Fishing Registration Port of Registry	Vessel Type Call Sign RSS/Official No.	Gross Tonnage Net Tonnage	Dimensions (ft.) Construction	Propulsion Power Unit/ Make	Build Date Build Location Build Yard	History
St. Davids LT90	Beam Trawler MLDT4 B10922	280 84	118 x 25 x 13 Steel	Diesel 8cyl 1600hp 1177kw Deutz	1980 Holland	Built as GO21 Elizabeth for W & J Lokker 1989 Bought by Colne Shipping Co. Ltd. 1989 Arrived at Lowestoft during July. Became LT90 St. Davids 1999 Re-engined in Holland 2000 A unit of the present Lowestoft fleet
St. Elizabeth Lowestoft	Trawler GAIJ 303299	622 186	167 x 30 x 14 Steel	Diesel 8cyl 1400hp 1030kw National	1962 Beverley Cook, Welton & Gemmell	Built as GY694 Northern Reward for Northern Trawlers Ltd. 1971 Transferred to Ross Trawlers Ltd. 1981 Bought by Colne Shipping Co. Ltd 1982/3 Converted for use as a SSV, renamed St. Elizabeth 1992 Sold during July and continued to be used as a SSV 1998 Renamed Veesea Eagle
St. Georges LT402	Trawler GPCH 181277	343 122	136 x 26 x 14 Steel	Diesel 6cyl 930hp Ruston	1946 Beverley Cook, Welton & Gemmell	Built as H318 Thorina for J. Marr & Son Ltd. 1948 Bought by J.V.Pronk NV, Ijmuiden. Registered as IJM33 1964 Sold to Claridge Trawlers Ltd. 1964 Arrived at Lowestoft on 21st. August. 1964 Registered as LT402 1965 Renamed St. Georges. 1967 Re-engined with a 8cyl 1100hp Ruston 1980 Used in filming of James Bond film " For Your Eyes Only " as the Maltese trawler VA402, during September 1984 Left Lowestoft on 7th June under tow for the shipbreakers
St. Georges LT59	Beam Trawler GDNT A18835	217 79	115 x 25 x 12 Steel	Diesel 6cyl 1100hp 809kw Deutz	1974 Holland	Built as Soli Deo Gloria 1980 Sold and became GO7 Jacob 1984 Sold to Colne Shipping Co. Ltd. 1984 Arrived at Lowestoft on 9th. March 1984 Became LT59 St. Georges in July 1985 Top Trawler under Skipper Athorn with earnings of £460,641 1995 Sold to W. Stevenson & Sons during January. 1995 Registered as PZ1053

Name Fishing Registration Port of Registry	Vessel Type Call Sign RSS/Official No.	Gross Tonnage Net Tonnage	Dimensions (ft.) Construction	Propulsion Power Unit/ Make	Build Date Build Location Build Yard	History
St.James LT492 Lowestoft	Trawler MIXV 181390	245 81	115 x 26 x 10 Steel	Diesel 6cyl 760hp Mirrlees	1957 Portsmouth Vosper	Built as GY421 Boston Vanguard for St. Andrews Steam Fishing Co. 1962 Bought by Vve Bon & Cie, La Rochelle. 1962 Became LR5003 Imprevu 1965 Sold to Kittiwake Ltd. 1965 Arrived at Lowestoft on 15th. November as Imprevu 1965 Became LT492 Suffolk Enterprise 1973 Transferred to Small & Co. (Lowestoft) Ltd. 1974 Sold to Claridge Trawlers Ltd. 1975 Renamed St. James during February 1980 Converted for use as a SSV 1986 Sold for scrapping in July 1986 Left Lowestoft on 21st August for the shipbreakers
St. James LT341	Beam Trawler GHWY A18980	289 90	112 x 25 x 13 Steel	Diesel 6cyl 1800hp 1343kw MaK	1974 Holland	1974 Launched as UK1 Albert for A.Romkes of Urk 1983 Lengthened from 112ft. to 126ft., tonnage 218 to 289 1986 Purchased by Colne Shipping Co. Ltd. 1986 Arrived at Lowestoft on 18th December 1994 Decommissioned and scrapped at Lowestoft
St. John LT7	Trawler GZLS 336038	241 82	121 x 26 x 11 Steel	Diesel 6cyl 1350hp Ruston	1969 Hessle Richard Dunston	Built for Claridge Trawlers Ltd 1969 Arrived at Lowestoft in April. 1986 Sold to Pesca Fisheries Ltd.. 1986 Left Lowestoft in November 1987 Became Pescafish I 1991 Became Badminton
St. John LT88	Beam Trawler MFAE9 A18853	312 93	120 x 26 x 14 Steel	Diesel 8cyl 1500hp 1103kw Deutz	1987 Holland	Built for Colne Shipping Co. Ltd. 1987 Arrived at Lowestoft on 16th March 1987 First Landing made on 2nd April 2000 A unit of the present Lowestoft fleet

Name Fishing Registration Port of Registry	Vessel Type Call Sign RSS/Official No.	Gross Tonnage Net Tonnage	Dimensions (ft.) Construction	Propulsion Power Unit/ Make	Build Date Build Location Build Yard	History
St. Kitts LT481	Trawler MHKB 166638	316 94	142 x 25 x 14 Steel	Diesel 8cyl 750hp Ruston	1941 Selby Cochrane	Launched as GY400 Le Royal for Grimsby Motor Trawlers Ltd. 1941 First successful distant water diesel trawler 1941 Completed as HMT Postboy for the Admiralty 1941 Given pennant number FY1750. In use on Anti Submarine duties 1943 Bought by Milford Steam Trawling Co. Ltd. (on charter to Navy) 1946 Returned by Navy to owner in July. 1946 Became M14 Milford Marquis 1949 At the end of the year, fishing 600 miles south of Las Palmas 1951 Sold to J.V.Pronk NV of Ijmuiden, became IJM35 Postboy 1964 Sold to Claridge Trawlers Ltd., became LT481 St.Kitts 1965 Top Trawler under Skipper E. Peek with earnings of £61,209 1975 During October suffered major engine damage, towed home 1976 Sold for scrapping after many months of being laid up 1976 Left on 29th Sept for the shipbreakers towed by St.Martin
St. Kitts Lowestoft	Trawler GMSE 305953	616 184	164 x 30 x 16 Steel	Diesel 8cyl 1280hp 945kw Mirrlees	1964 Beverley Charles Holmes	Built as LO94 Ella Hewett for Heward Trawlers Ltd. 1978 Bought by Claridge Trawlers Ltd. 1978 Arrived at Lowestoft on 2nd November 1978/9 Converted for use as a SSV, and renamed St. Kitts 1993 Sold during March and continued to be used as a SSV
St. Louis Lowestoft	Trawler GIAN 301694	596 224	166 x 30 x 16 Steel	Diesel 8cyl 1400hp 1030kw Mirrlees	1962 Beverley Cook, Welton & Gemmell	Built as H228 Lord Jellicoe for Lord Line Ltd. 1963 Registered as GY709 1966 Transferred to Northern Trawlers Ltd. 1971 Transferred to Ross Trawlers Ltd. 1981 Bought by Colne Shipping Co. Ltd. 1982 Converted for use as a SSV, and renamed St. Louis 1992 Sold and continued to be used as a SSV 1999 Reported as being sold for scrapping
St. Lucia LT362 Lowestoft	Trawler GHSU 302402	254 83	116 x 26 x 13 Steel	Diesel. 6cyl 845hp Ruston	1961 Hessle Richard Dunston	Built for Dagon Fishing Co. Ltd. 1964 Top Trawler under Skipper J. Peek with earnings of £54,884 1980 Converted during February for use as a SSV 1991 Sold for scrapping in June
St. Lucia P225	Beam Trawler MJRH2 A20244	373 111	124 x 28 x 15 Steel	Diesel 9cyl 2400hp 1765kw Deutz	1988 Holland	Built as P225 Cromer for Johnson's Sea Enterprises Ltd., 1994 Bought by Colne Shipping Co. Ltd. 1994 Renamed St.Lucia during April 2000 A unit of the present Lowestoft fleet

Name	Vessel Type	Gross Tonnage	Dimensions (ft.)	Propulsion	Build Date	History
Fishing Registration	Call Sign	Net Tonnage	Construction	Power Unit/	Build Location	
Port of Registry	RSS/Official No.			Make	Build Yard	

St. Luke	Trawler	391	140 x 28 x 11	Diesel	1961	Built as A574 Admiral Burnett for Parbell-Smith Ltd.
LT132	GLTJ	127	Steel	7cyl 1022hp	Aberdeen	1964 Sold to Maccofield Fishing Co. Ltd
Lowestoft	181295			Mirrlees	Hall Russell	1966 Sold to St.Andrews Steam Fishing Co. Ltd.
						1968 Transferred to BDSF and became FD14 Boston Lightning
						1976 Sold to Dagon Fishing Co. Ltd.
						1976 Arrived at Lowestoft on 4th December
						1977 Became LT132 St.Luke
						1978 Vessel abandoned and sank after an explosion on the 18th May
						1978 Located approximately 160 miles off Yorkshire coast
St. Luke	Trawler	619	164 x 30 x 16	Diesel	1961	Built as LO65 Robert Hewett for Heward Trawlers Ltd.
	GHNM	185	Steel	8cyl 1168hp	Beverley	1978 Sold to Claridge Trawlers Ltd
Lowestoft	302611			859kw Mirrlees	Cook, Welton	1978 Arrived at Lowestoft on 26th October
					& Gemmell	1978/79 Vessel converted for use as a SSV, became St. Luke
						1992 Sold during December and continued to be used as a SSV
						1998 Renamed Veesea Merlin
St. Mark	Trawler	434	140 x 28 x 13	Diesel	1960	Built as LO33 Captain Foley for the Iago Steam Trawler Co. Ltd.
LT327	GHFA	141	Steel	6cyl 1230hp	Aberdeen	1972 Became GY210 Boston Tristar
Lowestoft	302523			British Polar	John Lewis	1975 Arrived at Richards shipyard, Lowestoft, on 25th October
						1976 Sold to Colne Fishing Co. Ltd.,
						1976 Painted in Colne colours in July
						1976 Became LT327 St. Mark in October
						1980 Fully converted for use as a SSV
						1990 Sank after a collision on 6th August with Vikingbank
						1990 Located off north Norfolk coast in vicinity of Cromer
St. Mark	Beam Trawler	373	124 x 28 x 15	Diesel	1987	Built as P224 North Sea for Johnson's Sea Enterprises Ltd.
P224	MHPS	111	Steel	9cyl 2400hp	Holland	1994 Bought by Colne Shipping Co. Ltd.
	A20243			1765kw Deutz		1994 Renamed St. Mark during February
						2000 A unit of the present Lowestoft fleet
St. Martin	Trawler	254	116 x 26 x 13	Diesel	1961	Built for the Colne Fishing Co. Ltd.
LT376	GHTY	83	Steel	6cyl 845hp	Hessle	In later years used as a SSV
Lowestoft	302406			Ruston	Richard Dunston	1991 Sank on 10th. January
						1991 Located approximately 80 miles off the Lincolnshire coast

Name Fishing Registration Port of Registry	Vessel Type Call Sign RSS/Official No.	Gross Tonnage Net Tonnage	Dimensions (ft.) Construction	Propulsion Power Unit/ Make	Build Date Build Location Build Yard	History
St. Martin LT62	Beam Trawler MRNQ6 B12485	428 128	131 x 28 x 15 Steel	Diesel 9cyl 1799hp 1323kw Deutz	1991 Poland/ Holland	Built for Colne Shipping Co. Ltd. 1991 Arrived at Lowestoft on 17th November 1997 Top Trawler under Skipper J. Jonas with earnings of £789,000 1998 Top Trawler under Skipper J. Jonas with earnings of £798,650 2000 A unit of the present Lowestoft fleet
St. Matthew Lowestoft	Trawler GHJT 301645	540 164	165 x 30 x 16 Steel	Diesel 8cyl 1304hp Mirrlees	1960 Beverley Cook, Welton & Gemmell	Built as H219 Starella for J. Marr & Son Ltd. 1975 Sold to Boyd Line Ltd., renamed Arctic Rebel 1979 Sold to Colne Fishing Co. Ltd 1979 Converted for use as a SSV and renamed St. Matthew 1986 Sold for scrapping to Davies 1986 Left Lowestoft on 17th November for the shipbreakers
St. Matthew LT60	Beam Trawler MHDQ6 B12216	428 128	131 x 28 x15 Steel	Diesel 9cyl 1800hp 1324kw Deutz	1991 Yugoslavia/ Holland	Built for Colne Shipping Co. Ltd. 1991 Arrived at Lowestoft on 1st June 1992 Top Trawler under Skipper S. Jonas with earnings of £804,910 1996 Top Trawler under Skipper S. Jonas with earnings of £805,873 2000 A unit of the present Lowestoft fleet
St. Michael LT328	Beam Trawler GFSY A18970	206 86	113 x 25 x 12 Steel	Diesel 8cyl 1200hp 883kw Deutz	1974 Holland	Built as KW24 Pieter Jacob for C. Haasnoot of Katwijk 1979 Sold to Ymuiden and became Michael Bianca 1981 Re-engined. 1200hp Deutz replacing her 1200hp Anglo Belgiun 1982 Sold to H. Kramer of Urk and became UK227 Dirkje 1985 Sold to Colne Shipping Co. Ltd. 1985 Arrived at Lowestoft during December 1986 Fished as LT328 Dirkje until June 1986 1986 Became LT328 St. Michael on 14th June 1994 Sold for use as a houseboat on the Thames 1994 Left Lowestoft on 27th February, towed by tug Zephyr
St. Nicola LT83	Trawler GOXU 183932	349 141	145 x 26 x 13 Steel	Diesel 6cyl 1350hp Ruston	1949 Selby Cochrane	Built as M16 Milford Duchess for Milford Steam Trawling Co. Ltd. 1949 At the end of the year, fishing 600 miles south of Las Palmas 1954 Sold to French owners, became D11585 Joli- Fructidor 1968 Sold to Claridge Trawlers Ltd. 1968 Arrived at Lowestoft on 13th. July, towed by Jean-Vauquelin 1968 Became LT83 St. Nicola in December 1970 Re-engined 1971 First landing made in January 1985 Changed identity with newly acquired beamer Willem Adriana 1985 Sold for scrapping 1985 Left Lowestoft on 24th April under tow for the shipbreakers

Name / Fishing Registration / Port of Registry	Vessel Type / Call Sign / RSS/Official No.	Gross Tonnage / Net Tonnage	Dimensions (ft.) / Construction	Propulsion / Power Unit/ / Make	Build Date / Build Location / Build Yard	History
St. Nicola LT63	Beam Trawler PIPF A18836	241 88	111 x 25 x 12 Steel	Diesel 6cyl 1200hp 895kw Deutz	1974 Holland	Built as KW25 Willem Adriana 1982 Sold and became BM292 1985 Bought by Colne Shipping Co. Ltd. from Ladran Bay Trawlers 1985 Became LT63 St.Nicola 1995/6 Decommissioned and scrapped at Lowestoft
St. Patrick LT129 Lowestoft	Stern Trawler GUWV 362289	244 73	130 x 30 x 20 Steel	Diesel 6cyl 1650hp 1214kw Ruston	1975 Great Yarmouth Richards	Built for Claridge Trawlers Ltd., launched 12th August 1975 Landed record catch (LT) on 3rd Nov, 598 kits making £15,091 1976 Landed record catch (GY) on 9th Feb., 925 kits making £16,673 1976 Top Trawler under Skippers Besford/Martin, earnings £241,157 1977 Vessel mackerel fishing 1981 Top Trawler under Skipper Ketteringham, earnings £334,060 1983 Top Trawler under Skipper Ketteringham, earnings £383,712 1984 Top Trawler under Skipper Ketteringham, earnings £437,591 1986 Sold in August to J. Marr & Son and became H24 Gavina 1986/7 Re-engined after major engine failure. 1989 Purchased by Colne Group on 17th February 1989 Arrived back at Lowestoft on 9th March 1989 Converted for use as a SSV, renamed St. Patrick 1992 Sold during October for use as a SSV by other operators 1996 Became Viking Vixen
St. Paul Lowestoft	Trawler GHSX 301677	622 186	167 x 30 x 16 Steel	Diesel 8cyl 1400hp 1030kw Mirrlees	1961 Beverley Cook, Welton & Gemmell	Built as H344 Arctic Vandal for Boyd Line Ltd. 1973 Transferred to William Liston Ltd. 1976 Transferred to Boyd Line Ltd. 1979 Bought by Huxley Fishing Co. Ltd. 1979 Arrived at Lowestoft during May 1979 Transferred to Colne Fishing Co. Ltd. 1979/80 Converted for use as a SSV, renamed St. Paul 1993 Sold in January and continued to be used as a SSV
St. Peter LT 338	Beam Trawler PIQB A18977	227	113 x 25 x 12 Steel	Diesel 6cyl 1800hp 969kw MaK	1974 Holland	Built as UK158 Willem Jacob for A. van Urk of Urk 1979 Sold to M. Post of Urk and became UK253 Dageraad 1982 Sold to J. Meulmeester and became ARM16 Lenie-Adrianna 1986 Purchased by Colne Shipping Co. Ltd. 1986 Arrived at Lowestoft on 23rd. April 1986 1986 Became LT338 St. Peter 1994/5 Decommissioned and scrapped at Lowestoft

Name Fishing Registration Port of Registry	Vessel Type Call Sign RSS/Official No.	Gross Tonnage Net Tonnage	Dimensions (ft.) Construction	Propulsion Power Unit/ Make	Build Date Build Location Build Yard	History
St. Phillip LT144 Lowestoft	Stern Trawler GUYK 376312	244 73	130 x 30 x 20 Steel	Diesel 6cyl 1650hp 1214kw Ruston	1976 Great Yarmouth Richards	Built for Claridge Trawlers Ltd., launched 6th November 1976 Delivered in February 1978 Vessel mackerel fishing 1978 Top Trawler under Skipper Martin with earnings of £359,687 1986 Sold to Riverside Trawlers Ltd., Grimsby 1986 Left Lowestoft on 18th September for the Humber 1986 Renamed Kerry Kathleen 1988 Sold to Atlantean Fishing Co. Ltd., Sunderland 1989 Purchased by Colne Group on 31st March 1989 Arrived back at Lowestoft on 3rd April 1989/90 Converted for use as a SSV, renamed St.Phillip 1992 Sold on 25th November for use as a SSV by other operators 1998 Became Viking Vulcan
St. Rose LT82	Trawler GYVE 183931	349 141	145 x 26 x 13 Steel	Diesel 6cyl 1350hp Ruston	1949 Selby Cochrane	Built as M3 Milford Duke for the Milford Steam Trawling Co. Ltd. 1949 At the end of the year, fishing 600 miles south of Las Palmas 1955 Sold to French owners, became DI 1593 Jean Vauquelin 1968 Sold to Claridge Trawlers Ltd. 1968 Arrived at Lowestoft towing Joli-Fructidor on 13th. July 1968 Became LT82 St. Rose 1974 Re-engined 1985 Became Unda, engine removed in May. 1985 Sold for scrapping 1985 Left on 3rd July under tow for the shipbreakers
St. Rose LT300	Beam Trawler GYVE A18946	241 90	112 x 24 x 14 Steel	Diesel 6cyl 1200hp 895kw Deutz	1974 Holland	Built as KW22 Alida 1977 Became Lubbertje Kramer 1984 Became Alida 1985 Bought by Colne Shipping Co. Ltd. 1985 Arrived at Lowestoft on 18th. January. 1985 Became LT300 St. Rose 1996 Decommissioned and scrapped at Lowestoft in April
St. Simon LT304	Beam Trawler GFFS A18950	197 93	109 x 25 x 13 Steel	Diesel 6 cyl 1300hp 809kw Deutz	1974 Holland	Built as Stevn Willem for A. Visser 1978 Sold and became Andries De Vries 1981 Sold and became GO33 Cornellis Jannetje 1985 Sold to Colne Shipping Co. Ltd. 1985 Arrived at Lowestoft on 30th. March 1986 Top Trawler under Skipper Jonas with earnings of £567,627 1988 Re-engined in August with a 1300hp unit replacing the 1100hp 1998 Sold and renamed San Salvador 1998 Left Lowestoft on 26th February bound for Holland

Name / Fishing Registration / Port of Registry	Vessel Type / Call Sign / RSS/Official No.	Gross Tonnage / Net Tonnage	Dimensions (ft.) / Construction	Propulsion / Power Unit/ Make	Build Date / Build Location / Build Yard	History
St. Thomas LT8	Trawler GZLU 336043	241 82	121 x 25 x 11 Steel	Diesel 6cyl 1350hp 993kw English Electric (Ruston)	1969 Hessle Richard Dunston	Built for Claridge Trawlers Ltd. 1969 Arrived at Lowestoft in July 1970 Top Trawler under Skipper Hitter with earnings of £93,131 1975 Top Trawler under Skippers Besford/ Ketteringham 1975 Vessel earnings £188,275 1986 Sold to Pesca Fisheries Ltd. 1986 Left Lowestoft during November 1987 Became Pescafish II 1991 Became Blenheim
St. Thomas LT87	Beam Trawler MFZG7 A18852	312 93	120 x 26 x 14 Steel	Diesel 8cyl 1500hp 1103kw Deutz	1987 Holland	Built for Colne Shipping Co. Ltd. 1987 Arrived at Lowestoft on 16th May 1987 First landing made on 5th June 1987 Set new port landing record of 711kits grossing £58,334 1989 Top Trawler under Skipper Jonas with earnings of £762,809 1990 Top Trawler under Skipper Jonas with earnings of £867,886 1991 Top Trawler under Skippers Jonas/Athorn, earnings of £844,529 1999 Re-engined 2000 A unit of the present Lowestoft fleet
St.Vincent LT123	Trawler GGWU 301884	310 110	115 x 25 x 9 Steel	Diesel 6cyl 750hp 552kw Mirrlees	1959 Portsmouth Vosper	Built as FD193 Winmarleigh for Fleetwood N. W. Trawlers Ltd. 1967 Renamed Boston Hercules 1968 Sold to George Craig & Sons Ltd. 1969 Registered as A160 1970 Transferred to H. K. F. Trawlers Ltd. 1975 Sold to Claridge Trawlers Ltd. 1975 Arrived at Lowestoft on 1st. March. 1975 Became LT123 St.Vincent during May 1985 Used as a survey vessel during April 1985 Sold for scrapping to Henderson and Morez, Gravesend 1985 Left Lowestoft on 19th October for shipbreakers under tow
St.Vincent LT327	Beam Trawler PFDU A18969	249 130	125 x 25 x 11 Steel	Diesel 8cyl 1600hp 1177kw Deutz	1973 Holland	Built as the 112ft UK57 Johannes Post for F. Kramer of Urk 1980 Lengthened from 111ft. to 124ft. 1980 Re-engined from 1300hp to 1600hp 1985 Bought by Colne Shipping Co. Ltd. 1985 Arrived at Lowestoft on 7th. November 1986 Fished as LT327 Johannes Post until 5th February 1998 Sold and renamed Dorita 1998 Left Lowestoft on 27th March bound for Greece

| Name | Vessel Type | Gross Tonnage | Dimensions (ft.) | Propulsion | Build Date | History |
| Fishing Registration | Call Sign | Net Tonnage | Construction | Power Unit/ | Build Location | |
Port of Registry	RSS/Official No.			Make	Build Yard	
Tiberian	Trawler	302	124 x 25 x 12	Diesel	1961	Built as GY673 for Sir Thomas Robinson & Son (GY) Ltd.
	MEHY	95	Steel	12cyl 790hp	Selby	1976 Bought by Colne Fishing Co. Ltd.
Lowestoft	303281			Brons	Cochrane	1976 Arrived at Lowestoft on 29th October
						1976 Allocated fishing registration LT273
						1977 Converted for use as a SSV
						1977 Transferred to Dagon Fishing Co. Ltd.
						1978 Sold to Small & Co. (Lowestoft) Ltd in September
						1978 Became LT349 Suffolk Maid
						1981 Sold for use as a Caribbean trader
						1984 Broke from her moorings in St.Croix during a hurricane.
						1984 Substantially grounded
						1985 Many attempts to refloat Tiberian were made
						1986 Eventually refloated
						1986 The hulk of Tiberian was sunk to form an artificial reef.
Tobago	Trawler	168	108 x 21 x 10	Diesel	1950	Built as M128 Milford Countess for Milford Steam Trawling Co. Ltd.
LT182	MGZF	63	Steel	6cyl 420hp	Selby	1955 Bought by Colne Fishing Co. Ltd.
	183935			Ruston	Cochrane	1955 Became LT182 Tobago
						1964 Ran ashore near entrance to Lowestoft harbour
						1964 Refloated. Engine removed and sent to makers for reconditioning
						1964 Sold for scrap
						1964 Left on 8th October for the shipbreakers towed by Togo
Tobago	Trawler	211	104 x 23 x 10	Diesel	1959	Built as GY616 Saxon Venture for Alfred Bannister (Trawlers) Ltd.
LT165	MCIE	69	Steel	6cyl 720hp	Hessle	and Forward Steam Fishing Co. Ltd.
Lowestoft	301820			Ruston	Richard Dunston	1976 Sold to Colne Fishing Co. Ltd.
						1976 Arrived on 7th February at Lowestoft
						1976 Became LT165 Tobago during March
						1976 First landed as Tobago on 19th March
						1979 Converted for use as a SSV during November
						1986 Sold for scrapping to Cook Bros., New Holland
						1987 Left on 22nd January for the shipbreakers with Martinique
Togo	Drifter/Trawler	75	80 x 18 x 9	Diesel	1905	Built as steam drifter YH477 Togo for Fellows & Co. Ltd.
LT69	GJRN	28	Steel	3cyl 200hp	Great Yarmouth	1906 Bought by Admiral Fishing Co. Ltd., registered as LT609
	120341			Mirrlees	Fellows & Co.	1920 Sold to R. Balls and registered as YH248
						1935 Sold to Ling & Bird and registered as LT69
						1935 Converted to diesel power by LBS Engineering, Lowestoft
						1935 Transferred to Jubilee Fishing Co. Ltd.
						1958 Sold to Colne Fishing Co. Ltd.
						1964 Sold for scrapping
						1964 Left on 8th October for the shipbreakers towing Tobago

Name	Vessel Type	Gross Tonnage	Dimensions (ft.)	Propulsion	Build Date	History
Fishing Registration	Call Sign	Net Tonnage	Construction	Power Unit/	Build Location	
Port of Registry	RSS/Official No.			Make	Build Yard	

Togo	Trawler	174	94 x 23 x 9	Diesel	1965	Built as LT510 Boston Viking for BDSF
	GQVA	60	Steel	8cyl 528hp	Hessle	1966 Transferred to Fred. B. Parkes and Anthony B. Wilbraham
Lowestoft	306585			Blackstone	Richard Dunston	1970 Transferred to Weelsby Trawlers Ltd.
						1973 Sold to Connacht Trawlers Ltd., Galway and registered G110
						1974 Sold to Sir Basil Parkes and registered LT510
						1974 Arrived back at Lowestoft during June
						1974 Transferred to Pentode Ltd.
						1982 Sold to Ian Fraser Ker and became Fraser Viking
						1982 By October name had reverted to Boston Viking
						1983 Renamed Bob Reid II under the ownership of C.N.Scupham
						1984 Bought by Colne Shipping Co. Ltd.
						1984 Converted for use as a SSV and renamed Togo
						1991 Sold to Golden Arrow Boats (Dingle) Ltd., Tralee, Co. Kerry
						1991 Left Lowestoft on 27th. November
						1991 Reported as being used on charter work off Ireland
						1999 In use as diving support and charter vessel under the Belgian flag
Trinidad	Trawler	168	108 x 21 x 10	Diesel	1950	Built as M127 Milford Knight for Milford Steam Trawling Co. Ltd.
LT210	GKTZ	63	Steel	6cyl 420hp	Selby	1955 Sold to Clan Steam Fishing Co. (Grimsby) Ltd.
Lowestoft	183934			Ruston	Cochrane	1955 Arrived at Lowestoft on 10th. October.
						1955 Became LT210 Trinidad in November
						1957 Transferred to Drifter Trawlers Ltd.
						1970 In use as a SSV
						1976 Engine removed
						1976 Sold for scrapping to E.A.R.L. at Oulton Broad during May
Trinidad	Trawler	352	133 x 27 x 12	Diesel	1959	Built as FD173 Corena for J. Marr & Co. Ltd
	GDHU	124	Steel	7cyl 736hp	Selby	1970 Bought by Ranger Fishing Co. Ltd., Aberdeen.
Lowestoft	301876			Mirrlees	Cochrane	1972 Sold to Forward Motor Trawlers Ltd. used as a SSV
						1978 Sold to Colne Fishing Co. Ltd.
						1978 Arrived at Lowestoft on 22nd March
						1978 Fully converted for use as a SSV.
						1978 Renamed Trinidad in June
						1986 Sold for scrapping during December

Name / Fishing Registration / Port of Registry	Vessel Type / Call Sign / RSS/Official No.	Gross Tonnage / Net Tonnage	Dimensions (ft.) / Construction	Propulsion / Power Unit/ / Make	Build Date / Build Location / Build Yard	History
Tritonia LT188	Drifter/Trawler GYWN 149246	123 50	92 x 20 x 9 Steel	Diesel 6cyl 335hp Ruston	1930 Oulton Broad John Chambers	Built as a steam drifter/trawler for the Herring Fishing Co. Ltd., 1936 Sold to S. J. Tripp 1939 Requisitioned by the Admiralty in November 1940 Assigned pennant number FY973 and in use as a minesweeper 1945 Sold to Vigilant Fishing Co. Ltd. 1946 Returned from Admiralty in January 1957 Sold to Mitchells Tritonia Ltd. 1957/8 Converted to diesel power by Richards Ironworks 1975 Sold to Colne Fishing Co. Ltd. during November 1976 Sold for scrapping at Oulton Broad
Una LT198	Drifter/Trawler MGFT 183965	114 52	85 x 22 x 9 Steel	Diesel 6cyl 230hp Mirrlees	1950 Hessle Henry Scarr	Built as LT198 Waveney Queen for WHSN Co. Ltd. 1960 Sold to Drifter Trawlers Ltd. Renamed Una 1969 Vessel offered for sale at £8500 during April 1970 Sold to Pounds (Shipbreakers & Shipbrokers) Ltd. 1970 Left Lowestoft on 17th December
Unda LT270	Drifter/Trawler GNZN 183983	114 52	85 x 22 x 9 Steel	Diesel 6cyl 230hp Mirrlees	1952 Hessle Henry Scarr	Built as LT270 Underley Queen for WHSN Co. Ltd. 1960 Sold to Drifter Trawlers Ltd. Renamed Unda 1969 Vessel offered for sale at £8500 during April 1970 Sold to Pound (Shipbreakers & Shipbrokers) Ltd 1970 Left Lowestoft on 17th December 1972 Sold to Mr. R. Francis, Duncan, British Columbia. 1997 In Spanish ownership
Unda Lowestoft	Trawler GYVE 183931	349 141	145 x 26 x 13 Steel	Diesel 6cyl 1350hp Ruston	1949 Selby Cochrane	Refer to LT 82 St.Rose for history
Vera Creina LT758	Drifter/Trawler GQLD 130009	80 35	83 x 18 x 9 Steel	Steam 32hp(180ihp) Compound Crabtree	1911 Gt.Yarmouth Crabtree	Built for W. J. Head and G. F. Wright 1913 Transferred to Head & Wright Ltd. 1946 Sold to Jubilee Fishing Co. Ltd. 1953 Sold to Colne Fishing Co. Ltd. 1954 Sold for scrapping.

Name	Vessel Type	Gross Tonnage	Dimensions (ft.)	Propulsion	Build Date	History
Fishing Registration	Call Sign	Net Tonnage	Construction	Power Unit/	Build Location	
Port of Registry	RSS/Official No.			Make	Build Yard	

Waddington	Trawler	230	109 x 24 x 9	Diesel	1962	Built as GY680 for Peter Sleight Trawlers Ltd.
LT79	GHYA	76	Steel	6cyl 622hp	Hessle	1975 Sold to Colne Fishing Co. Ltd.
	303286			Ruston	Richard Dunston	1975 Arrived at Lowestoft during August
						1975 Registered as LT79
						1981 Converted for use as a SSV
						1984 Re-engined
						1991 Sold for scrapping in October.
Willa	Drifter/Trawler	84	75 x 20 x 7	Diesel	1935	Built for LT (1934) Ltd.
LT43	GQLG	34	Steel	5cyl 150hp	Lowestoft	1946 Sold to Universal Trawlers Ltd., Fleetwood
Lowestoft	162976			Ruston	Richards	1947 Sold to G. D. Claridge
						1949 Transferred to Colne Fishing Co. Ltd.
						1955 Transferred to Dagon Fishing Co. Ltd.
						1955 Lengthened to 82 x 20 x 7. Gross tonnage to 83.
						1955 Re-engined with 5cyl 220hp Ruston
						Extensively modernised in early 1960's
						1971 In use on SSV duties
						1986 Sold for scrapping to G T Services, Barking
						1986 Left Lowestoft on 27th June for the shipbreakers
Willem Adriana	Trawler	349	145 x 26 x 13	Diesel	1949	Refer to LT83 St. Nicola for history
	GOXU	141	Steel	6cyl 1350hp	Selby	
Lowestoft	183932			Ruston	Cochrane	
Yellowfin	MFV	115	92 x 22 x 10	Diesel	1945	Refer to LT282 Alorburn for history
LT282	MAWZ	42	Wood	6cyl 360hp	Par	
	182019			Ruston	Frank Curtis	
Yellowtail	MFV	119	92 x 23 x 10	Diesel	1945	Refer to LT326 Maravanne for history
LT326	MAYN	43	Wood	6cyl 360hp	Looe	
	180190			Ruston	Frank Curtis	

The first vessel owned by Mr. G. D. Claridge and the Colne group of companies to be named *Ala* was a small 1933 built Lowestoft trawler. Purchased in 1945 by Mr. Claridge, she is seen here in the late 1930s in the colours of her previous owner, the LT (1934) Co. Ltd. *Ala* was one of the first vessels acquired by him, and after three years service was sold to the Government of India.

The former Admiralty *MFV1542* was destined to be the second *Ala* owned by Mr. Claridge. Built in 1944, she was purchased in 1948. In 1956, *Ala* was sold to Torbay Trawlers Ltd. and became the *William Allen. LT393 Ala* is seen leaving Lowestoft on the 30th October 1948

The first large truly successful diesel powered British trawler was *GY153 British Columbia*. She was built by Richards in 1935 for Grimsby Motor Trawlers, and became the second diesel trawler to have been owned by that company. Their first diesel trawler was built by Cochrane in 1920. In some respects, Grimsby could be said to have lead the way in adopting diesel propulsion in trawling. She was purchased by Mr. Claridge after war service, during which she became the *Guava*. In 1949, she had her original name of *British Columbia* reinstated, and was registered as *LT404*. This view of *British Columbia* was taken in 1935 and shows her ready for launching, complete with Grimsby registration. This photograph is taken from her builder's archives.

Another 1935 view of this remarkable vessel, taken from her builders archives. She is at the fitting out quay of Richards in the Inner Harbour at Lowestoft.

The *British Columbia* is seen here in her final form when in the ownership of the Colne subsidiary company of Clan Steam Fishing Co. (Grimsby) Ltd. She sank in the North Sea during September 1957, following a collision with the American destroyer *Purdy*.

Another former MFV to serve in the Colne fleet became the *LT267 Grasby*. She is seen here entering Lowestoft on return from a fishing trip. *Grasby* was part of the Colne fleet from 1951 until 1955 when she was sold.

One of the vessels to carry the name *Eta* was the former *MFV1506*. Rigged for drifting we seen her here as *LT400,* crossing the Waveney Dock during the home fishing of 1954. In 1956 the *Eta* was sold, and during 1957 became the *Arduous*. She was hulked in 1969 and later buried.

Of the eight small trawlers built in the 1930s by Richards shipyard at Lowestoft, six eventually passed into the ownership of Mr. Claridge and the Colne group of companies. The last to be completed was *LT236 Celita* in 1939. During her life she was extensively modernised with reconstruction of part of her hull in the 1950s, and the fitting of a new wheelhouse in the 1960s. *Celita* is seen here entering Lowestoft harbour in essentially the form in which she was built. In 1970, she was sold for scrapping at Oulton Broad.

The tragic loss of the trawler *LT73 Guava* with her crew of eleven is vividly remembered today. We see her here on the 14th November 1951, approaching Lowestoft harbour during her short life as a fishing vessel. The *Guava* was built in 1945 as a minesweeper, and after conversion to a trawler operated out of Lowestoft from 1949, until her disappearance in January 1953.

Based on the design of the *British Columbia*, the *British Guiana* and *British Honduras* were built by Cochrane at Selby, the *Guiana* in 1936 and the *Honduras* in 1937. They were both built for Grimsby Motor Trawlers Ltd. After war service, both were briefly under Lowestoft ownership before moving to Milford Haven. By 1950, they were back at Lowestoft and owned by Claridge Trawlers with the registrations *LT52* and *LT134*.

(Above)
LT52 British Guiana leaves Lowestoft on another fishing trip in 1955. She was sold for scrapping at Oulton Broad in 1968.
(Left)
LT134 British Honduras approaches the harbour entrance at Lowestoft. In the Trawl Dock can be seen a "Short Blue" steam trawler, and on Columbus Buildings, the name of "Consolidated Fisheries". *British Honduras* was sold for scrapping at Sheerness in July 1968.

(Below) An unusual vessel belonging to the Colne subsidiary, Clan Steam Fishing Co. (Grimsby) Ltd., was the drifter *A57 Cedargrove.* She was acquired by Mr. Claridge when her owners, the Clan Steam Fishing Co., were taken over in 1952. She is officially recorded as belonging to the Lowestoft company until 1960. *Cedargrove* is seen here leaving Anstruther bound for Great Yarmouth and the East Anglian herring season. She took part in this fishery until the mid 1950s.

(Above) Some of the crew bid farewell to their relations as they leave for East Anglia. It is believed that the vessel never visited Lowestoft.

Both views are from the Scottish Fisheries Museum collection.

At a late stage in their lives, these four steam drifters were all owned by the Colne group of companies. These historic photographs were all taken before these vessels became part of the Colne fleet. They had all gone to shipbreakers yards by the mid 1950s. (Top Left) *LT758 Vera Creina* is seen on the beach at Bacton on the 9th October 1939. It cost in the order of £800 to salvage her. (Top Right) *LT756 Buckler* was recorded leaving Lowestoft in the early 1930s. (Bottom Left) During her life, the Admiralty "standard" drifter *LT407 Calm Waters* had been given three different Scottish fishing registrations, those of Aberdeen, Inverness and Fraserburgh. She became a Lowestoft registered vessel in the late 1940s, and is here seen approaching Lowestoft on 29th October 1949. (Bottom right) Another "standard" owned by Mr. Claridge was *LT239 Flora Taylor.* The early part of her life was spent under Scottish ownership, and after this she had a period in North Shields ownership. In 1930, she was registered at Lowestoft.

Photographs of the Scottish registered herring drifter *PD388 Equity I* taken in 1952 when in the ownership of the Colne Group are quite rare. We see her here during the home fishing heading out of Lowestoft for the herring grounds. Within weeks she was re-registered as *LT343*, and later renamed *Madame Prunier*. In 1953, she was sold to Pevensey Castle Ltd. one of the Small & Co. group of companies.

Built in Holland by Gebreeders Boot at Liederdorp in 1916, the *Patria* was Lowestoft owned between 1930 and 1954. She received her Lowestoft registration of *LT178* in 1930. In 1947, *Patria* won the Prunier Trophy with a landing of 253 crans. Colne Fishing Co. Ltd. was her last owner at Lowestoft, and she was sold for scrapping in 1954.

Early views of vessels that later in life became part of the Colne Group are always interesting. (Above) We see the *Patria* as a drifter entering Lowestoft harbour. (Left) In the early 1930s, rigged for trawling and entering the bridge channel at Lowestoft

During the early 1950s three of the small "Ala" class trawlers in the Colne fleet had new raked stems and foc'sle heads fitted. The three were *Willa*, *Rewga* and *Celita*. This fine view by John Wells shows *LT236 Celita* leaving on a fishing trip after the work had been carried out. Later all of the "Ala" class had new modern style wheelhouses fitted.

During 1957, a Milford Haven fishing vessel owner was taken over and the Colne Group inherited two steam drifter/trawlers. The Company was the Drifter Trawlers Co. Ltd., and the vessels were the 1920 built *R355 Lady Luck* (Left), and the 1914 built *R129 Mill o' Buckie* (below). They are both seen here with their Ramsgate fishing registrations at Milford Haven, and before becoming Colne vessels. The view of the *Lady Luck* was recorded on the 9th July 1955.

(Above) After suffering engine trouble, *LT282 Alorburn* is towed into Lowestoft by the tug *Ness Point. MFV1530* became *A614 Alorburn* in 1948, and was purchased by Clan Steam Fishing in 1952 when she was registered as *LT282*. In 1958 she was renamed *Yellowfin* and in 1970 she was sold for non-fishing purposes. *Ness Point* was built in 1937 for the LNER and was scrapped in 1963.(Right) One of the two MFVs that were sold to South Africa in 1962 was *LT68 Albacore*, built in 1943 as *MFV1516*. After a period as the Hull owned and registered *Kristin*, she was bought by Mr. G. Claridge in 1949. Initially renamed the *Albercore*, she later became the *Albacore*. Both trawlers are seen in their pre 1957 condition, and before being extensively modernised.

LT326 Maravanne was one of the four former MFVs in the fleet that were modernised in the late 1950s. She is seen here leaving Lowestoft in the early 1960s, after being modernised and renamed *Yellowtail*. Her remains can still be seen at the western end of Lake Lothing. For a number of years, she was in a partially submerged condition near the lock at Oulton Broad.

(Above) For a few years a number of the steel diesel powered Colne vessels had black painted topsides, complete with white stripe. This black was later changed to grey. Some vessels such as *LT64 Montserrat*, were delivered new from their builders with this attractive colour scheme. (Right) Built for the West Hartlepool Steam Navigation Co. Ltd. in 1952 at the Hessle shipyard of Henry Scarr, *LT270 Underley Queen* was sold to the Colne subsidiary of Drifter Trawlers Ltd. in 1960. One of three similar vessels purchased at the time, she became the *Unda*. The other two vessels were the *Ira* and *Una*. All three were sold in late 1970 to a dealer at Portsmouth. We see her here leaving on a fishing trip in the mid 1960s.

During 1960, Claridge Trawlers Ltd. purchased three small German built trawlers. Their appearance made these vessels unique at Lowestoft. Purchased from the Irish Sea Fisheries Board, they were originally built for German owners in Bremerhaven in 1948 and 1949. They retained their former names of *Loch Lein, Loch Lorgan* and *Loch Laoi* under Colne Group ownership.

(Above) *LT334 Loch Lein* is seen in the Outer Harbour, with the now demolished South Pier Pavilion in the background. When purchased, only *Loch Lein* was in her original condition. The other two had new wheelhouses fitted whilst in Irish ownership. In 1967, she was sold and eventually ended her days in New Zealand. She sank in 1988. (Right) One of the other two, *LT335 Loch Lorgan* leaves Lowestoft on a fishing trip. Both *Loch Lorgan* and her sister ship, the *Loch Laoi,* left Lowestoft in June 1970 for a shipbreakers yard at Blyth.

The "Fish" class trawlers were long serving members of the Colne fleet. Richard Dunston Ltd. built all the members of the class between 1955 and 1961, to a standard basic design. However, later members of the class had variations in hull design incorporated into them, and some were fitted with a more powerful engine. In the early days of her life, the first of the class, *LT186 Kingfish,* leaves Lowestoft on a fishing trip. She was sold for scrapping in 1986.

The eighth member of the "Fish" class, *LT340 Silverfish*, leaves Lowestoft in 1961 shortly after delivery. When comparing this photograph with that on the previous page, the design differences between the early and later vessels of the class are quite apparent. The *Silverfish* was sold and left the fleet in 1987.

Returning from a fishing trip in March 1964, *LT182 Tobago* ran aground close to the Lowestoft harbour entrance. Built as the *Milford Countess* for the Milford Steam Trawling Co. Ltd in 1950, she had joined the Colne fleet in 1955. After being refloated, *Tobago* was later sold for scrapping. See the next page for the start of *Tobago's* final voyage.

(Left) Built as a Yarmouth steam drifter in 1905, the *Togo* was converted from steam to diesel propulsion in 1935 when she was also given the registration *LT69*. She came into Colne ownership in 1958, and after a long and successful career as a trawler, was sold for scrapping in 1964. *Togo* is seen here leaving her home port on a fishing trip.

(Right) On the 8th October 1964, the *Togo* left Lowestoft for the shipbreakers, taking with her the engineless remains of *LT182 Tobago*. The funnel of the *Tobago*, complete with the Company houseflag, can be seen lying on the deck. *Tobago's* engine was removed before she was sold for scrap, and later reconditioned and reused.

(ABOVE) LANDING A TRAWLERS CATCH
(RIGHT) SELLING THE FISH BY AUCTION

(ABOVE) LANDING AND SORTING

(BELOW) AT SEA ABOARD A COLNE SIDE TRAWLER

(ABOVE) PREPARING FOR SEA-
TAKING ON ICE SUPPLIED BY
THE LOWESTOFT ICE CO.

(ABOVE) PREPARING FOR SEA-
CHECKING AND REPAIRING
THE GEAR

In the mid 1970s, Claridge Trawlers Ltd. took delivery of two new stern trawlers which were built at the Richards (Shipbuilders) Ltd. yard at Gt. Yarmouth. The two vessels were *LT129 St. Patrick* completed in 1975, and *LT144 St. Phillip* completed in 1976. The second of the pair, the *St. Phillip,* is seen here leaving Lowestoft in the late 1970s. By 1986, both vessels had left the Lowestoft fleet, having been sold to two different owners on the Humber. In the spring of 1989, they were back under the control of the Colne Group. Both were converted at Den Helder for use as safety standby vessels. Since the early 1990s, they have been sold a number of times, and at the time of writing are still operational as standby vessels. Photographs of these vessels after conversion can be found elsewhere in this book.

By the 1970s, many trawlers had ceased fishing and had been converted to standby vessels for use in support of the offshore oil and gas industry. *LT67 Anguilla* was one of the vast number of vessels to undergo conversion, and she is seen here as a typical example of a former trawler in the standby role. Built by Cochrane in 1959 at Selby, the *Anguilla* was sold in 1986, and after a period under Milford Haven ownership became a sailing vessel in the Caribbean.

A traditional view at Lowestoft during the festive season, when all the trawlers are in port. Christmas 1979 saw this group, representing three different Lowestoft owners, together in the Waveney Dock. The vessels are *LT372 Suffolk Craftsman* owned by Small & Co., the Colne Fishing Co. trawler *LT309 Port Vale*, and *LT 509 Boston Viscount* owned by the Boston Group. Both the *Suffolk Craftsman* and the *Port Vale* are former Grimsby trawlers; the *Suffolk Craftsman* was previously *GY672 Priscillian*. The *Port Vale* was purchased by Colne Fishing in 1978 and kept her original name. The much-appreciated tradition of all the trawlers and their crews being home for Christmas continues at Lowestoft, when the Colne fleet of beam trawlers can be found either at Riverside or in the Trawl Dock.

The Aberdeen trawler *A163 Burnbanks* was one of many vessels bought by the Company for conversion to a standby vessel. She is seen here on the fishing grounds, and before being purchased by Colne Shipping in 1982. *Burnbanks* was launched in 1959 as the *Midlothian,* but completed as the *Lothian Leader.* In Colne ownership, *Burnbanks* became the *Culebra.* She was sold for scrapping, and left Lowestoft on the 24th April 1985. This fine view is from the Scottish Fisheries Museum collection.

BYGONE BEAMERS - The Company has owned a total of 21 beam trawlers, these four are some of those that have been disposed of. (Top Left) *LT328 St. Michael.* Sold for further use in a non-fishing role in 1994. (Top Right) *LT335 St. Andrew.* Decommissioned and scrapped in 1994. (Bottom Left) *LT338 St. Peter.* Decommissioned and scrapped in 1994. (Bottom Right) *LT300 St. Rose.* Decommissioned and scrapped in 1996.

VESSELS OWNED BY COLNE COMPANIES

This lists in alphabetical order, the final names of vessels that have been, or are vessels of the Colne fleet. It does not necessarily reflect the name by which a vessel was predominantly known, and does not include chartered vessels.

Final Name	Previous Names	Period In Fleet
Abaco	Judaean	1976-1985
Ala	Herbert Crampin	1987-1997
Ala		1945-1947
Ala	MFV1542	1948-1956
Ala	Sean Claire	
	Pinegarth	1974-1986
Albacore	Albercore	
	Kristin	
	MFV1516	1949-1962
Aldershot		1978-1987
Anegada	Ross Curlew	1981-1991
Anglerfish		1961-1987
Anguilla		1959-1986
Antigua		1957-1986
Aruba	Hawkflight	1975-1991
Aylesby	MFV1579	1951-1951
Bahama		1957-1986
Barbados		1958-1985
Barbuda	Jacklyn	1975-1991
Barnsley		1978-1992
Bermuda		1955-1980
Bermuda	Ross Mallard	1980-1992
Blackburn Rovers		1978-1987
British Columbia	Guava	
	British Columbia	1946-1957
British Guiana	Milford Knight	
	Sunlit Waters	
	British Guiana	1949-1968
British Honduras	Milford Baron	
	Peaceful Star	
	British Honduras	1950-1968
Buckler		1952-1954
Caicos	Ross Kelly	
	Kelly	1982-1987
Calm Waters	Olive Tree	
	Moyra	
	Dew	1953-1954
Carlisle		1978-1987
Cedargrove		1952-1960
Celita		1947-1970

Final Name	Previous Names	Period In Fleet
Celita	Tippermuir	
	Ocean Trust	1980-1987
Colne Hunter	Prince Phillip	1984-1991
Colne Kestrel	Boston Kestrel	1984-1992
Colne Phantom	Boston Phantom	1984-1992
Crystal Palace		1978-1992
Culebra	Burnbanks	
	Lothian Leader	
	Midlothian	1984-1985
Cuttlefish		1959-1981
Desirade	Ross Kittiwake	1982-1991
Dominica	Ross Cormorant	1982-1991
Enderby	MFV1565	1951-1952
Eta	MFV1506	1948-1956
Eta	Brenda Fisher	1979-1986
Eta	Clevelandman	
	Anglianman	
	Motorman	1989-In Fleet
Exuma	Brave Buccaneer	
	Boston Buccaneer	1975-1991
Fertile		1946-1954
Fiskerton		1975-1981
Flora Taylor	Moonset	1952-1954
Gillingham		1978-1987
Gordon David	Hannah Christine	1995-1998
Grasby	MFV1534	1951-1955
Grayfish		1961-1974
Grenada		1955-1986
Guana	London Town	1984-1987
Guava	MMS	1949-1953
Gula		1946-1986
Hosanna		1975-1976
Huddersfield Town		1978-1992
Inagua	Ross Eagle	1982-1992
Ira	Bentley Queen	1960-1970
Jamaica	Star of Scotland	1959-1976
Jamaica	Boston Crusader	
	Broadwater	1976-1986
Kennedy	Boston Britannia	1974-1986
Kingfish		1955-1986
Lady Luck		1957-1957

Final Name	Previous Names	Period In Fleet
Lass O' Doune		1945-1946
Loch Laoi	Hermann Leymann	1960-1970
Loch Lein	Rheinland	1960-1963
Loch Lorgan	Martin Schilling	1960-1970
Madame Prunier	Equity I	1952-1953
Mardyke	John Henry	1970-1973
Martinique	Thessalonian	1976-1987
Merbreeze		1975-1976
Mill O' Buckie		1957-1957
Montserrat		1959-1987
Mustique	Ross Heron	1981-1991
Nevis	Ross Kelvin	
	Kelvin	1981-1987
Notts Forest		1978-1991
Pagona	Ross Hawk	1982-1991
Patria	Atlantic	1954-1954
Port Vale		1978-1986
Real Madrid		1978-1981
Rewga		1947-1970
Rewga	Ocean Dawn	1984-1987
Rockfish		1956-1986
Ross Cormorant	Dominica	1958-1983
Ross Heron	Mustique	
	Olivean	1976-1982
Rotha		1947-1986
Saltrou	Clova	1982-1987
Samarian		1976-1979
Sawfish		1959-1987
Scampton		1975-1991
Silverfish		1961-1987
Snapper	Red Snapper	
	Sea Monarch	
	Herm Coast	
	MFV1532	1952-1962
Spearfish		1956-1983
Spurs		1978-1991
SSAFA		1975-1987
St. Andrew	Elze Willem Fokke	1986-1994
St. Anne	Lord St. Vincent	1980-1992
St. Anthony		1999-In Fleet

Final Name	Previous Names	Period In Fleet
St. Christopher	Pietertje Elisabeth	1986-1994
St. Claude	Boston Shackleton Haselbech	1982-1986
St. Claude	Eben Haezer	1989-In Fleet
St. Croix	Parkroyd	1976-1986
St. Croix	Atlas Maarten	1985-1994
St. Davids	Allan Water	1964-1980
St. Davids	Northern Gift	1980-1987
St. Davids	Elizabeth	1989-In Fleet
St. Elizabeth	Northern Reward	1981-1992
St. Georges	Thorina	1964-1984
St. Georges	Jacob Soli Deo Gloria	1984-1995
St. James	Imprevu Boston Vanguard	1974-1986
St. James	Albert	1986-1994
St. John		1969-1986
St. John		1987-In Fleet
St. Kitts	Milford Marquis Postboy Le Royal	1964-1976
St. Kitts	Ella Hewett	1978-1993
St. Louis	Lord Jellicoe	1981-1992
St. Lucia		1961-1991
St. Lucia	Cromer	1994-In Fleet
St. Luke	Boston Lightning Admiral Burnett	1976-1978
St. Luke	Robert Hewett	1978-1992
St. Mark	Boston Tristar Captain Foley	1976-1990
St. Mark	North Sea	1994-In Fleet
St. Martin		1961-1991
St. Martin		1991-In Fleet
St. Matthew	Arctic Rebel Starella	1979-1986
St. Matthew		1991-In Fleet
St. Michael	Dirkje Michael Bianca Pieter Jacob	1985-1994
St. Nicola	Willem Adriana	1985-1995
St. Patrick		1975-1986
St. Patrick	Gavina	1989-1992
St. Paul	Arctic Vandal	1979-1993
St. Peter	Lenie Adriana Dageraad Willem Jacob	1986-1994

Final Name	Previous Names	Period In Fleet
St. Phillip		1976-1986
St. Phillip	Kerry Kathleen	1989-1992
St. Rose	Alida Lubbertje Kramer Alida	1985-1996
St. Simon	Cornellis Jannetje Andries De Vries Stevn Willew	1985-1998
St. Thomas		1969-1986
St. Thomas		1987-In Fleet
St. Vincent	Boston Hercules Winmarleigh	1975-1985
St. Vincent	Johannes Post	1985-1998
Tiberian		1976-1978
Tobago	Milford Countess	1955-1964
Tobago	Saxon Venture	1976-1987
Togo		1958-1964
Togo	Bob Read II Boston Viking Fraser Viking Boston Viking	1984-1991
Trinidad	Milford Knight	1955-1976
Trinidad	Corena	1978-1986
Tritonia		1975-1976
Una	Waveney Queen	1960-1970
Unda	Underley Queen	1960-1970
Unda	St. Rose Jean Vauquelin Milford Duke	1968-1985
Vera Creina		1953-1954
Waddington		1975-1991
Willa		1947-1986
Willem Adriana	St. Nicola Joli Fructidor Milford Duchess	1968-1985
Yellowfin	Alorburn MFV1530	1952-1970
Yellowtail	Maravanne MFV1529	1952-1970

Notes

A) There are a number of other vessels known to have been owned by Mr. G. Claridge or the Colne companies for a brief period of time, and not used operationally as fishing vessels. These include the following: -
1. *MFV1053*. Became the *Anita*, and was sold in 1949 to W. Stevenson & Sons, whilst still being converted for fishing. Later became *PZ193 W & S* and in 1969, *SA14 Julie Ann*.
2. Steam drifter/trawler *Lord Duncan*. Built 1920, scrapped 1954 after sinking in harbour.
3. Steam trawler *Ouse*. Built 1900, scrapped 1954. Towed *Lord Duncan* to shipbreakers.
4. Steam trawler *Tanager*. Built 1910, scrapped 1955.

B) As standby vessels, the *St. Patrick* and *St. Phillip* were owned by Colne Shipping in the early 1990s. Hence the double entry for both vessels.

C) A small number of vessels were renamed very late in their lives, usually before they were sold for scrapping. This was to release a name for reuse on another Company vessel. Four examples of this practice were: - *LT82 St. Rose* became *Unda*, *LT83 St. Nicola* became *Willem Adriana*, *LT314 Dominica* became *Ross Cormorant* and the standby vessel *Mustique*, (formerly *Olivean*) became *Ross Heron*.

D) Details of vessels, including any notified changes of identity are listed elsewhere in this book.

One of the early vessels in the Company building programme of 1955 was *LT130 Grenada.* We see her here entering Lowestoft just after midday on the 13th April 1973.

The first of the "Fish" class trawlers was *LT186 Kingfish,* built in 1955. This view shows her returning from a fishing trip on the 4th August 1973.

The small trawlers of the "Ala" class were used for many years as standby vessels after their fishing days had ended. As standby vessels, three of the class are seen here, the 1935 built *Willa (LT43)*, the 1936 built *Gula (LT179)* and the 1937 built *Rotha (LT208)*. In later years, vessels such as these would no longer be considered suitable for this work, due to the introduction of more stringent regulations concerning standby vessels. All remaining members of the class received new wheelhouses in the early 1960s. Some vessels of the "Ala" class were over 50 years old when finally withdrawn from service, and sold for scrapping. (Right) New raked stems, were fitted to three of the class in the mid 1950s. One of the three, the *Willa*, is seen here in the Trawl Dock. (Below Left) *Rotha* is about to leave the Trawl Dock for another spell of providing support to the offshore oil and gas industry. This view was recorded on the 6th April 1973. (Below Right) Her period of standby duty having been completed, the *Gula* is seen returning to port on the 8th August 1973.

Lady Cora was a much-travelled vessel that for a few months in 1974, carried Colne colours. Built in 1956 by John Lewis at Aberdeen as *GY333 Boston Valetta,* she was transferred in 1961 to Acadia Fisheries of Halifax, Nova Scotia and became the *Acadia Fin-Fare.* In 1968 she returned to Europe and became *LT256* and had her original name reinstated. After a number of changes in ownership, she was sold in 1973 to Dunedale Ltd., of Douglas in the Isle of Man. *Lady Cora* was sold for scrapping at Oulton Broad in 1976.

(Above) *Lady Cora* in the Inner Harbour at Lowestoft complete with the Colne house flag. This scene was recorded on the 5th February 1974.

(Right) Leaving Lowestoft for a period of duty as a standby vessel on the 25th June 1974.

After her fishing days at Lowestoft had ended, *LT64 Montserrat* served as a standby vessel for a number of years. In 1987, she was sold to Anglo-Spanish interests. *Montserrat* was built in 1959 for Huxley Fishing Co. Ltd., by Cochrane at Selby. In this scene, she had just entered Lowestoft on the 8th March 1975.

Perhaps more than any other British fishing company, the Colne group of companies owned over the years a number of historic British fishing vessels. One such vessel was the Cochrane built *LT481 St. Kitts*. The story of this trawler could easily fill a book. She was completed during the last war, having been ordered as Britain's first diesel powered distant water trawler, by one of the pioneers of diesel propulsion, Grimsby Motor Trawlers. After war service and being owned by two other owners, she was purchased by Claridge Trawlers in 1964. After problems with her ageing main engine, she was sold for scrapping in 1976. She is seen here on the 12th June 1973.

Richards (Shipbuilders) Ltd. at their Great Yarmouth yard, launched two stern trawlers for the Colne subsidiary of Claridge Trawlers Ltd. in 1975. (Above Left) Mrs. Claridge launched the *St. Phillip* on the 6th November. (Above Centre) A view of the launching party with Mr. G. Claridge on the right of the photograph. (Above Right) *St. Phillip* glides into the water. (Below) Earlier in the year, on the 12th August, the *St. Patrick* had been launched. She is seen here a few minutes after entering the water.

This superb view of *LT376 St. Martin,* just returned from a fishing trip, was recorded on the 13th August 1975 in the Waveney Dock. After a successful fishing career, she was converted for standby work and sank in early 1991.

The large sidewinder *LT132 St. Luke* sank after an explosion, probably caused by a mine in 1978. She was previously *A574 Admiral Burnett,* and later *FD14 Boston Lightning. St. Luke* was built in 1961 by Hall Russell at Aberdeen, and purchased by Dagon Fishing Co. Ltd. in 1976.

One of the three trawlers purchased from Peter Sleight Trawlers in 1975, *GY166 Scampton,* lies in the Trawl Dock shortly after arrival. Under Colne ownership she became *LT110* and retained her original name. Built in 1962 at Hessle, *Scampton* became a standby vessel in 1981 and was sold for scrapping in 1991. This scene was recorded on the 23rd September 1975.

Seen here off Lowestoft on the 15th October 1968, *LT232 Spearfish* suffered a unique fate when she was shelled by the Royal Navy. Built in 1956 as one of the first generation of "Fish" class vessels, she was sunk by gunfire from *HMS Tartar* after being involved in a collision and becoming a navigational hazard. At the time she was employed as a standby vessel.

Built at Grimsby in 1958 for the Clan Steam Fishing Co. (Grimsby) Ltd., *LT312 Barbados* and her sister ship the *Dominica,* were of the "Improved Bermuda" class. Here we see *Barbados* entering Lowestoft in April 1973. She was sold for scrapping in 1985 after her engine had been removed.

This view of the *Barbados* shows her being assisted into port by the tug *Ala* on the 25th June 1974. This tug was previously the *Pinegarth,* later to become *Sean Claire.* She joined the Colne fleet in February 1974, and capsized off Lowestoft in January 1986. The wreck was destroyed by explosives six months later.

LT67 *Anguilla* was built for the Clan Steam Fishing Co. (Grimsby) Ltd. at Selby in 1959. She is seen here off Lowestoft and heading for the fishing grounds on the 4th July 1973. *Anguilla* was sold in 1986 after serving for a number of years as a standby vessel.

The first tug purchased by the Colne Group was the *Mardyke*. Built as the *John Henry*, she was purchased after having had three owners. These included the Port of London Authority and R. E.Trim. *Mardyke* was declared a total loss after grounding on Corton Sands in 1973. In this 1972 scene, having just completed landing, the Lamprell owned trawler *Jadestar Glory* is being moved by *Mardyke* across the Waveney Dock.

The diesel powered trawler *A425 Star of Scotland* was in Scottish terms, an historic vessel. She was built for Walker Steam Fishing Co. Ltd. in 1947 by Hall Russell at Aberdeen, and paved the way for the modernisation of the Aberdeen fleet. The *Star of Scotland* was purchased by the Dagon Fishing Co. Ltd. in 1959, and became *LT185 Jamaica* in 1960. For a number of years, she was the largest trawler working out of Lowestoft. *Jamaica* was converted for use as a standby vessel in 1972 and was sold for scrapping in 1976.

(Above) The *Jamaica* entering Lowestoft on the 8th August 1975 when in use as a standby vessel. (Left) A close up view of the wheelhouse and funnel of *Jamaica* as *A425 Star of Scotland*, shortly after arrival at Lowestoft. This unique scene was recorded on the 27th December 1959 at the North Quay. This is now the location of the Lowestoft Container Terminal.

Prior to becoming a Colne trawler, the *St. James* led an interesting life. Built in 1957 as the Grimsby registered *Boston Vanguard* by Vospers at Portsmouth, she was sold into French ownership in 1962. During 1965, Kittiwake Ltd., a subsidiary of Small & Co. (Lowestoft) Ltd., purchased her and she became *LT492 Suffolk Enterprise.* She was transferred into the ownership of the parent company in 1973.

During late 1974, the Colne Group purchased *Suffolk Enterprise* and in 1975, renamed her *St. James.* Converted for standby work in 1980, *St. James* was sold for scrapping in 1986. She left Lowestoft for the breakers yard of G. T. Services on the 21st August.

(Above) Much interest is shown in seeing vessels in the colours of a former owner. In the ownership of Small & Co., *Suffolk Enterprise* leaves Lowestoft for the fishing grounds in 1967.

(Left) Early in the morning of the 4th August 1976, *St. James* heads for the harbour entrance at Lowestoft.

The trawler *LT157 Boston Buccaneer* was built by Richards at Lowestoft in 1961 for the Boston Group. She was sold in 1973 to C. V. Eastick, and became the *Brave Buccaneer.* After being purchased by the Huxley Fishing Co. Ltd. in 1975, she was renamed *Exuma.* Used as a standby vessel by the Colne Group, *Exuma* left Lowestoft bound for a shipbreakers yard on the 16th January 1992, after being sold for scrap. We see her here leaving Lowestoft in 1976 for standby duty in the North Sea.

Aruba was built as *A530 Hawkflight* in 1961 by John Lewis for Hawkstone Fishing. She is seen here entering the Trawl Dock, after arriving home from standby duty on the 15th September 1976. *Hawkflight* was sold by Hawkstone in 1971, and was in Irish ownership until 1973, when she joined the *Exuma* in the ownership of C .V. Eastick. Bought by Huxley at the same time as the *Exuma, Aruba* was initially used for fishing, before being converted for standby duties. She was sold for scrap and left Lowestoft in August 1991, bound for a shipbreakers yard.

Many Grimsby trawlers were purchased in the 1970s, one of which was *GY616 Saxon Venturer.* We see her here on the 15th February 1976 in the dry dock, being prepared to become the Colne trawler *LT165 Tobago.* After fishing for 3 years, *Tobago* was converted for standby work. She was sold for scrapping in January 1987.

LT 142 Bahama makes a fine sight as she leaves her home port on the 13th June 1973. Built at Hessle she was delivered new in 1957 from her builders with black topsides.

VIEWS FROM THE WHEELHOUSE OF A
SIDE FISHING TRAWLER ON THE
FISHING GROUNDS WITH THE TRAWL
BEING HAULED
As the net is hauled in, the cod end slowly rises
to the surface. The cod end, laden with fish, is
hauled on board and swung over the deck

The cod end is swung over the deck and positioned over the pounds. It is then undone and the fish cascade into the pounds. Crew members are later seen sorting and gutting the fish, after which it is washed and passed into the hold where it is packed in ice and stored.

LT210 Trinidad was withdrawn from service following a D.O.T. survey. On the 13th May 1976, when this scene was recorded, she was at the North Quay, after her engine had been removed, and shortly before her last journey to the shipbreakers yard at Oulton Broad. *Trinidad* was originally the Milford Steam Trawling Co. vessel *M127 Milford Knight.* Also visible in this scene is the now preserved *LT412 Mincarlo.*

Trinidad was built in 1950 by Cochrane at Selby. She was purchased in 1955 by Clan Steam Fishing, a Colne subsidiary, and in 1957 was transferred to another subsidiary, Drifter Trawlers Ltd. She is seen here leaving Lowestoft on a fishing trip shortly after joining the Colne fleet in late 1955.

A number of Aberdeen registered trawlers joined the fleet, one of which was *A160 Boston Hercules*. She was formerly the Fleetwood registered *Winmarleigh*, and became *LT123 St. Vincent* under the ownership of Claridge Trawlers, a Colne subsidiary. *St.Vincent* was sold for scrapping and left Lowestoft under tow in October 1985. She was recorded here entering Lowestoft as the *Boston Hercules* on the 3rd May 1975. The name *St. Vincent* was later used on a beam trawler.

On the 21st October 1976, *GY445 Samarian* arrived at Lowestoft after purchase by Colne. During 1977 she was converted for standby work and by the end of that year had developed major engine problems. She was towed home and in 1979 sold for scrap. This superb view shows her off Lowestoft, late in the afternoon of the 31st October 1976.

A truly atmospheric scene at Aberdeen in 1979. *GY699 Ross Mallard* was purchased by Drifter Trawlers Ltd. during 1980, and arrived at Lowestoft on the 14th June. By the end of that year, she had become the standby vessel *Bermuda,* the second Colne vessel to carry that name. Built by Cochrane at Selby in 1962, she had at least five changes of ownership before becoming a Lowestoft vessel. *Bermuda* was sold for scrapping in April 1992, but was resold for further use in a non-fishing capacity.

One of the many Consolidated Fisheries Group trawlers to be purchased by Colne in 1978 was *GY674 Real Madrid.* Seen in the dry dock at Lowestoft on the 22nd July 1979, she was used as a source of spare parts and then sold for scrapping in 1981.

Several distant water trawlers joined the Colne fleet for conversion to high specification standby vessels. *GY694 Northern Reward* was purchased in 1981 and after conversion became the 300 Hospital Class standby vessel *St. Elizabeth*. She was sold in 1992. Beverley shipbuilders Cook, Welton and Gemmell built *Northern Reward* in 1962 . This view shows the *Eta*, a former Grimsby tug, with the former Grimsby trawler at Lowestoft on the 24th January 1981.

Another of the former Consolidated Group trawlers to move to Lowestoft in 1978 was *GY484 Port Vale*. On the 25th November 1978 she is seen approaching the harbour entrance as a trawler, with her Lowestoft registration of *LT309*.

After conversion to a Colne 250 North Atlantic Survivor Class vessel, *Port Vale* leaves Lowestoft to go on station. Each of the eleven North Atlantic Class carried twin high-speed rescue craft mobilised by electro-hydraulic davits. Also they had bulwark entry doors with adjacent fast deployment scrambling nets, and 18 foot clear space aft for helicopter pick up operations. In addition they were fitted with twin oil dispersant spraying booms supplied with 5.5 metric tonnes capacity bulk storage tanks. A very comprehensive range of communication and navigation equipment was carried. Below decks, there were 27 cabin bunks, 38 seats in aft accommodation and 185 seats in the forward lower saloon. The medical bay was situated in the forward lower section with sophisticated medical and anti-hypothermia back up adjacent to all areas.

This fine view shows the trawler *Barnsley* entering Lowestoft on the 10th April 1979. She entered service with Colne in 1978 and was sold for scrapping in 1992

An early arrival amongst the large distant water trawlers that made Lowestoft their home in the 1970s and 1980s, was *LO94 Ella Hewett.* One of the last "Short Blue" trawlers, she is seen arriving at Lowestoft on the 2nd November 1978. *Ella Hewett* was converted into the Colne 300 Hospital Class vessel *St.Kitts* and sold by Colne in 1993.

Undoubtedly the trawler that has been seen by more people than any other, is the Colne Group's *St. Georges.* Formerly the Hull trawler *Thorina* this classic side trawler was chosen to play the part of the British intelligence gathering ship *St. Georges* in the James Bond film " For Your Eyes Only ". The film is still shown around the world and in 1999, was shown on British television. With her fictitious fishing registration, *St. Georges* leaves Lowestoft on the 2nd September 1980 on her way to the filming location. Contrary to information published in a number of books, the *St. Georges* was not scrapped immediately after the filming. She returned to Lowestoft and continued her fishing career until 1984, when she was sold for scrapping.

The *Fiskerton*, one of three trawlers purchased from Peter Sleight Trawlers at Grimsby in 1975, leaves Lowestoft on the 14th November 1978. She was sold for scrapping in 1981.

The Lowestoft shipbuilder Richards Ironworks built many diesel powered drifter/trawlers between 1949 and 1960, for owners in Lowestoft and Great Yarmouth. In the year 2000, very few of these vessels still exist. Two of these flexible vessels, originally the *Ocean Dawn* and *Ocean Trust*, came into the ownership of the Colne Group and were used as standby vessels. They were renamed *Rewga* and *Celita*. One of these the *Rewga*, has regained her original name and once again can be seen in British waters as the *Ocean Dawn*. The other vessel, the *Celita*, was sold to Anglo-Spanish owners by Colne and became the *Belton*.

YH377 Ocean Trust was built for Bloomfields of Great Yarmouth in 1957, and passed into Lowestoft ownership in 1963. She was later sold to Scottish owners, and after 17 years of fishing and use as a standby vessel, she was purchased by the Colne Group.

(Above) In the early 1980s, *Celita* leaves Lowestoft for a spell of standby duty in the North Sea.

(Left) As part of the Small & Co. fleet, *Ocean Trust* leaves Lowestoft with other drifters on a Sunday morning in 1964.

After the demolition of the Great Eastern Railway built marketing and processing hall in 1984, the Waveney Dock took on a very different look. This view of two Colne Shipping vessels, shows the area before the present processing hall was built. The vessels are the stern trawler *LT129 St. Patrick*, later to become the standby vessel *Viking Vixen*, and *LT251 St. Croix*, previously the Aberdeen registered *Parkroyd*. The *St. Croix* was sold for scrap in January 1986.

Of the large number of trawlers built at Richards shipyard at Lowestoft after the last war, very few served in the Colne fleet. Most were converted for standby use, but one spent many years fishing, before it too, became a standby vessel. This trawler was the *Barbuda*, recorded here leaving Lowestoft on the 7th June 1984 on a fishing trip. She was built as one of Richards Standard 91foot Class trawlers in 1962 for Jackora Ltd., as the *Jacklyn*. After being transferred into the ownership of the White Fish Authority in 1975, she was purchased by Colne Fishing. Renamed *Barbuda* in 1976, she spent nine years fishing for the Company before becoming a standby vessel. *Barbuda* was sold for scrapping in 1991.

Richard Dunston at Hessle built two sisterships, the *St. Thomas* and the *St. John*, for Claridge Trawlers in 1969. They were the last side trawlers built for the Colne fleet. Both vessels passed into Anglo Spanish ownership in 1986. (Below) The first to arrive in April was the *St. John*, seen here later in life in the Waveney Dock. (Left) The *St. Thomas* arrived in July and under Skipper Hitter was top trawler the following year. We see her here leaving for the fishing grounds on the 31st March 1979.

A number of tugs have been owned by the Colne Group since 1970. Shown here are two of these vessels, both of which no longer exist.

(Right) The *Ala* capsized off Lowestoft in January 1986, and the wreck was later blown up. She was built as the *Pinegarth* for Rea Towing in 1961 and in 1973 was sold and became the *Sean Claire*. During 1974, *Sean Claire* was purchased by Colne and renamed *Ala*. She is seen here as the *Sean Claire,* in the Inner Harbour at Lowestoft. This scene was recorded on the 10th May 1974. The CWS canning factory on the right of the photograph has been completely demolished and the site levelled. A new business park is being built there. The now closed shipyard of Richards (Shipbuilders) Ltd., is on the left of the photograph with two distant water trawlers of the Boston fleet receiving attention. In 2000, the shipyard is used for offshore fabrication work, but could be "redeveloped" as a shopping and leisure centre by a developer in association with Waveney District Council.

(Left) Purchased by Colne in 1979, the Grimsby tug *Brenda Fisher* became the *Eta* in August of that year. She is seen here on 20th March 1983 making for the harbour entrance at Lowestoft, after assisting with the departure of one of the many rig modules built in the town. After her engine had been removed she was scrapped on the shores of Lake Lothing in 1986.

The Aberdeen trawler and standby vessel *A417 Clova,* was a typical example of the large number of vessels purchased by the Colne Group, to supplement its standby fleet. The *Clova* was built in 1960 at the Aberdeen shipyard of John Lewis, and was purchased by Colne Shipping in 1982 when she became *Saltrou*.

(Above) In 1987, *Saltrou* was sold, and became the Warbler Shipping Company vessel *Dawn Saviour*. She is seen here leaving her home port. In 1993, she was sold by Warbler to Middle East interests.

(Right) *Clova* off Aberdeen, and in the colours of a previous owner, British United Trawlers. This view is from the Scottish Fisheries Museum Collection.

FD256 Boston Kestrel was purchased by Colne Shipping in 1984, after she had been chartered for a few years by the Company. In March 1985 she became *Colne Kestrel.* This fine view of her, taken in 1985, includes features of the Inner Harbour at Lowestoft which no longer exist. These include on the left of the photograph, Mortons Canning Factory, and on the right, ships being built at Richards (Shipbuilders) Ltd. yard. On the 23rd January 1992, *Colne Kestrel* left her home port for the shipbreakers.

A number of trawlers previously owned by the Boston Group entered service with the Colne Group in the early 1980s. Seen here in the colours of the Boston Group, are two of those vessels.

A vessel with a complicated history is the Hessle built former trawler and standby vessel *Togo,* now a diving and sport-fishing vessel. She is one of the few former Lowestoft side trawlers to survive into the 21st century, and which are still sea going. In this view, recorded on the 14th February 1982 she is the *Fraser Viking,* a name by which she was briefly known. Built as *LT510 Boston Viking* in 1965, she was owned by several different companies before becoming the Colne Shipping standby vessel *Togo* in 1984. *Togo* was sold by Colne in 1991 and visited Lowestoft in 1999.

The well-known trawler *LT714 Boston Shackleton* is seen leaving her homeport after the Christmas break on the 27th December 1974. Formerly *GY628 Haselbech*, she was purchased by the Colne Group in 1976 and renamed *St. Claude*. She left Lowestoft after being sold for scrap on the 15th July 1986.

The importance to the economy of Lowestoft of the Colne Group, and maritime related industries in general, is illustrated in these photographs. These views of the recent past show different aspects of harbour life and include fishing, the offshore oil and gas industry, tourism and shipbuilding. Trawlers and offshore standby vessels of the Colne Group can be seen, together with yachts in the Yacht Basin and Sir Richard Branson on the *Virgin Atlantic II.* This record breaker was built at the shipyard of Brooke Yachts in the town.

(Above) *Virgin Atlantic II* arrives at Lowestoft on the 8th July 1986, complete with her owner on board. A large number of Colne standby vessels can be seen, the most prominent being *Rewga*, built as the Yarmouth drifter/trawler *Ocean Dawn.* (Right) The 24th December 1976 and most of the Colne Fleet are in port. Many are seen in this view of the Trawl Dock, but a number of Company standby vessels would be at sea on station.

151

The former side trawler *GY492 Ross Curlew* was in use as a standby vessel, before she became the Colne vessel *Anegada*.
She is seen here off Lowestoft on the 27th September 1981, shortly after entering service with her new owner.
The *Anegada* was sold for scrapping in December 1991.

The Colne Shipping Company bought their first beam trawler in 1984. The vessel was the *Jacob*, a 1974 built Goedereede registered vessel.

On the 15th April 1984, she was in the Trawl Dock together with the tug *Ala* and had been painted in the Company colours with her new registration. She was still awaiting formal acceptance of her new name, *St. Georges*, but the letters had already been welded on. The trawler had arrived at Lowestoft on the 9th March.

LT59 St. Georges off Lowestoft. She was sold in January 1995 to W.Stevenson & Sons.

Built as *M16 Milford Duchess* by Cochrane in 1949, *LT83 St. Nicola* joined the Colne fleet in 1968 after several years in French ownership. She is seen here on the 12th July 1984, leaving her home port for another fishing trip. Elsewhere in this book, this fine example of a classic sidewinder is seen leaving on her last voyage to the shipbreakers, as the *Willem Adriana*.

LO33 Captain Foley was built for Iago Steam Trawling in 1960. During 1972, she became *GY210 Boston Tristar,* and in 1976 was purchased by Colne Fishing. She became *LT327 St. Mark* in October 1976, and after fishing for approximately three years, was converted for standby work. As a standby vessel, she is seen here at the Lowestoft Container Terminal. In August 1990, following a collision, *St. Mark* sank off Cromer.

Another vessel lost whilst in service as a standby vessel was the former trawler *LT376 St. Martin.* Built for the Colne Group in 1961 at Hessle, she sank off Lincolnshire in 1991, after many years service as a trawler and a standby vessel. In this view *St. Martin* is moored in the Trawl Dock, with the now demolished Ross Group building in the background.

The present Colne Shipping tug joined the fleet in 1989, and is the second Company tug to carry the name *Eta*.
In this spectacular scene, captured at 2105hrs on the 12th June 1997, she is seen leaving Great Yarmouth with
Skipper Richard Fiske in charge. *Eta* is returning to Lowestoft after assisting with barge movements in the river.

(Top Left) Colne was the last owner of three very well known Lowestoft drifter/trawlers. The names of *Hosanna, Merbreeze* and *Tritonia* were part of the British fishing scene for almost half a century. Perhaps they are best known for their many years of service as steam powered herring drifters, when they followed the shoals around the British Isles. All three were converted to diesel power in the late 1950s and early 1960s. After purchase by Colne, anything of value was removed from them, and they were taken to the shipbreakers at Oulton Broad in 1976. They are seen here at the North Quay at Lowestoft on 15th December 1975.

(Top Right) *LT167 Hosanna* heads out of Lowestoft on 1st August 1973. At that time, she was in the ownership of Scattan Ltd.

(Bottom Left) Just before being sold for scrap, the much-loved classic sidewinder *LT83 St. Nicola* had her name exchanged with that from a new addition to the Colne fleet. She was one of a number of vessels treated in this way, and became the *Willem Adriana* for the last weeks of her life. Together with the *Culebra*, she is seen leaving Lowestoft for the last time, heading for a shipbreakers yard and cutting up. *St. Nicola* was originally the Milford Haven trawler *Milford Duchess.* The *Culebra* was the Aberdeen trawler *Burnbanks* before joining the Colne fleet. The date is 24th April 1985.

The standby vessel *Abaco* suffered a severe fire whilst at sea off the Humber on 17th July 1984. The crew took to the liferaft and were picked up by a Danish trawler, later they were passed to the Colne vessel *Blackburn Rovers*. They landed at Lowestoft on the 18th July. *Abaco* was towed back to Lowestoft and later sold for scrapping, leaving on the 16th November 1985. She was formerly the trawler *GY644 Judaean*.

(Top and Bottom Left) 22nd July 1984 - North Quay. The badly fire damaged wheelhouse and superstructure of the *Abaco*.

(Top Right) 19th July 1984 - Bridge Channel. Upon reaching her home port, *Abaco* is towed through the bridge and into the Inner Harbour.

The Colne standby vessel *Spurs* in the Inner Harbour at Lowestoft. She joined the Colne fleet in 1978, and was allocated the fishing registration *LT303*. However, she never did fish for the Company. *Spurs* was sold for scrap in 1991 after ten years service as a 250 North Atlantic Class vessel.

There is widespread interest in the fate of trawlers once their fishing days are finally over. A fine selection of former trawlers is featured in the next few pages.

Before joining the Colne fleet, these standby vessels were: -

(Top Left)   GY706 Blackburn Rovers

(Top Right)   GY680 Waddington

(Bottom Right) FD252 Boston Phantom

More former trawlers working out their final years as part of the vast Colne fleet. As fishing vessels these were: -

(Top Left)   *GY60 Ross Kelvin*

(Bottom Left)   *H219 Arctic Rebel*

(Bottom Right)   *GY138 Prince Phillip*

This group of standby vessels at the North Quay were previously, from left to right-

GY683 Crystal Palace

FD173 Corena

H261 Lord St. Vincent

FD256 Boston Kestrel

Awaiting their fate at the Brooke Marine shipyard, three standby vessels that as distant water trawlers were, from left to right: -

LO65 Robert Hewett

H261 Lord St. Vincent

LO94 Ella Hewett

A superb view of the *St. Phillip* taken shortly after her conversion from a stern trawler to a high specification standby vessel in 1990.
The sight of a Colne standby vessel in the vicinity of an offshore structure such as that seen in the photograph was very common between
the late 1960s and early 1990s. *St. Phillip* is now the *Viking Vulcan* owned by Viking Standby Ships Ltd. and registered at Montrose.

(Top Left) *LT304 St. Simon* was a long serving member of the Colne beamer fleet. She entered service with the Company in 1985 and was sold in 1998. *St. Simon* was built in 1974 as the *Stevn Willem*, and left Lowestoft as the *San Salvador* on 26th February 1998.

(Bottom Left) With a net fouling her propeller, *LT341 St. James* enters her home port in 1987 with the assistance of a tug. Built as *UK1 Albert* in 1974, she came into Colne Shipping ownership in December 1986. *St. James* was one of the beam trawlers decommissioned and broken up at Lowestoft in 1994.

(Bottom Right) One of the Colne owned Portsmouth registered pair, *P224 St. Mark* was built as the *North Sea* in 1987. This large beamer joined the Lowestoft fleet in February 1994 and is seen here on 9th November 1997.

Two views of the Colne Shipping float in the 1982 Lowestoft Carnival procession. Earlier that year, the parent company had changed its name from Colne Fishing Co. Ltd. to Colne Shipping Co. Ltd. following a reappraisal of the Groups interests

The strangest addition to the fleet occurred in 1982 when the three masted sailing ship *St. Peter* arrived. The crew of pirates represented European counties such as Holland, Spain, Belgium and France. Britannia, complete with shield, sucked a baby's dummy!

Here *St. Peter* is waiting to set sail from the procession assembly point, on a voyage through the town centre. The message was "Britannia rules the waves, while EEC pirates waive the rules".

The Colne Shipping Co. Ltd. offices in Waveney Road

After many years LBS Engineering vacated these Hamilton Road premises in 1998

Adjacent to the southbound A12 road and the Waveney Dock is the Lowestoft Ice Co.

The fuel depot of East Coast Oil Wharves is situated in Hamilton Road

From their present premises at Riverside, Colne subsidiary LBS Engineering has undertaken contract work and also provided assistance to visiting trawlers.

(Right) The Anglo Dutch owned beam trawler *BCK43 Quo Vadis* at Riverside on 29th June 1998. Various work was carried on this vessel including slipping at Laundry Lane on the 6th July.

(Below) When the Dutch owned beam trawler *GY57 Eben Haezer* docked at Lowestoft on 11th February 2000, LBS Engineering was called upon to assist the crew with the trawler's gear.

For many years, Colne has provided towage facilities with their numerous tugs. The present tug is the second one to be named *Eta*. She is often called upon to perform interesting and unusual tasks, often working with the Putford tug *Planter*. Under Skipper Richard Fiske, a former top Lowestoft trawler skipper, this versatile vessel is seen undertaking three typical tasks. (Below Top) 9th March 2000 - Assisting at the launch of the *Sharon Rose* at the Great Yarmouth shipyard of Richards. (Below Bottom) 14th January 2000 - The 185ft. replica Mississippi-style paddle steamer *Dixie Queen* underwent a major refit at Lowestoft between December 1999 and February 2000. *Eta* is seen towing *Dixie Queen* in the Inner Harbour at Lowestoft.

(Above) 17th May 1999 - Assisting the large Swedish Rock Carrier *West Sky* into the Waveney Dock. Note the superb condition of the *Eta*.

East Coast Oil Wharves are the fuel supplies division of the Colne Group. Their road tankers are frequently seen delivering fuel to various vessels. As well as supplying the Colne fleet, the Company has a wide customer base. Three different Colne customers are shown here. (Bottom Left) 26th July 1999 - Lowestoft is home to one of the most important tug fleets in Britain. Tugs of the Klyne fleet are frequently in port. These included Britain's largest tug, the *Anglian Monarch*, seen at the rear of the Colne vehicle. The tug nearest the camera is the *Lady Laura*. (Top Right) 26th July 1999 - Lowestoft is also home to the major offshore standby and supply vessel owners, Putford Enterprises. The *Putford Puffin* is seen at Town Quay, Lowestoft. (Bottom Right) 15th August 1984 - Many occasional visitors to the port such as the *Sagacity*, a vessel of the F. T. Everard & Sons Ltd. fleet, are East Coast customers.

The Group has disposed of over one hundred and forty vessels. Four of these vessels are featured here. (Top Left) *Togo* was sold in 1991. She is seen here at Lowestoft in 1999 in use as a charter vessel. *Togo* was originally *LT510 Boston Viking*. (Top Right) *LT340 St. Christopher* was decommissioned and cut up in 1994. (Bottom Left) *LT327 St.Vincent* was sold in 1998, reportedly for further use as a fishing vessel. (Bottom Right) The standby vessel *St. Patrick* was sold in 1992. She later became the *Viking Vixen*.

During May 1999 the main engine of *LT87 St. Thomas* was replaced, and other major work carried out on the vessel at the Laundry Lane slip at Lowestoft.

(Top Left) Awaiting collection, the original engine stands covered with a tarpaulin. (Top Right) A general view of *St. Thomas* on the slip. (Bottom Right) The vessel at sea.

Unlike some fishing ports that rely heavily on fish supplies arriving overland by road, Lowestoft's role as a major 21st century fishing port and centre, is primarily dependent on landings by trawlers such as these. (Top Left) 16th March 1998- *LT714 St. Claude* leaves Lowestoft for the fishing grounds. (Top Right) 9th December 1998-In dense fog *P225 St. Lucia* nears the harbour entrance. (Bottom Left) 15th April 1999-*LT90 St. Davids* arrives home from Holland after a refit and being re-engined. (Bottom Right) Christmas 1999-Trawlers wait to land at three of the landing berths.

(Top Left) 29th March 1999 - The vessel's visitor open day. (Top Right) Part of the engine room. (Bottom Left) The main engine. (Bottom Right) The view from the top of the wheelhouse.

(Top left) The crew - left to right - Chief Engineer Jimmy Tusting, Deckhand Clifford Warren, Mate Gavin Athorn, Deckhand Graham Crickmore, and Deckhand John Cooke.
(Top Right) Skipper Roly Reynolds observing the trawl being shot. (Bottom Left) The trawl being shot. (Bottom Right) Hauling, with Deckhands Warren and Crickmore in attendance.

(Top Left) Mate Gavin Athorn and Deckhand John Cooke preparing to release the Cod End. (Top Right) Shaking the Cod End. (Bottom Left) Deckhand Graham Crickmore tying the knot after clearing the nets. (Bottom Right) On the fishing grounds - The Man from the Ministry, Chris Garrod of the CEFAS Laboratory at Lowestoft measuring fish taken from the catch.

General deck scenes with the *St. Anthony* on the fishing grounds

(Top Left) Some of the catch on the conveyor before sorting. (Right) Deckhand John Cooke gutting. (Bottom Left) The Mate and two of the Deckhands sorting the catch.

(Top Left) Well before dawn, the *St. Anthony* is ready to land at Berth 5 in the Waveney Dock. (Top Right) Part of the catch in the Fish Hold. (Bottom Left) A view from the trawler of landing in progress at Lowestoft's modern fish market. (Bottom Right) Some of the catch on the quayside, seen from the wheelhouse balcony

(Top Left) Inside the Processing Hall with *St. Anthony* just visible through the door. (Top Right) Skipper Roly Reynolds (far right), with four of the crew after the trip. (Bottom Left) Off to sea again. (Bottom Right) *St. Anthony* at sea.

ST. DAVIDS - MARCH 2000

SELECT BIBLIOGRAPHY

Down The Harbour 1955-1995 by Malcolm White (White-1998)
40 years of fishing vessels, owners, the harbour and shipyards at
at Lowestoft

A Century of Fishing by Malcolm White (White-1999)
Fishing from Great Yarmouth and Lowestoft 1899-1999

Almost a Century of Shipbuilding (Richard Dunston Ltd.)
British Coastal Ships, Tugs & Trawlers by G. Mayes (Ian Allan-1974)
British Trawlers by H. M. Le Fleming (Ian Allan-1958)
Eighty Years of Shipbuilding by L. E. Richards (Richards Ironworks-1956)
Fishing Vessels of Lowestoft by V. Duncan (Woodside-1952)
Fishing News Various Editions (EMAP)
From Steam to Stern by D. L. King (PLRS-1975)

Lloyds Register of Shipping Various Editions (Lloyds)
The First Hundred Years by Charles Goodey (Boydell-1976)
Maritime Directories Various Editions (HMSO)
Merchantile Navy List Various Editions (HMSO)
Olsen's Fisherman's Nautical Almanack Various (Dennis & Sons Ltd.)
PLRS Newsletters Various Editions (PLRS)
The Lowestoft Fleet List 1978 by D. L. King (PLRS-1978)